THAT YOU MAY LIVE

How the 10 Commandments
Lead to Human Freedom

DARRELL JOHNSON

Published in 2023 by Canadian Church Leaders Network
#101-1155 Thurlow St., Vancouver, BC, V6E 1X2
www.ccln.ca

Design by Arielle Ratzlaff

Unless otherwise noted, Scripture quotations are taken from the NEW AMERICAN STANDARD BIBLE®, Copyright © 1960,1962,1963,1968,1971,1972,1973,1975,1977,1995 by The Lockman Foundation. Used by permission.

Library and Archives Canada Cataloguing in Publication

Title: That you may live : how the 10 commandments lead to human freedom / Darrell Johnson.
Names: Johnson, Darrell W., 1947- author.
Description: Includes bibliographical references and index.
Identifiers: Canadiana 20230505732 | ISBN 9781990331060 (softcover)
Subjects: LCSH: Ten commandments. | LCSH: Christian life.
Classification: LCC BV4655 .J64 2023 | DDC 241.5/2—dc23

**Interested in studying the
10 Commandments with a group?**

Download a Group Discussion Guide to go
alongside this book at **DARRELLJOHNSON.CA**

(Includes questions, readings, and prayer
invitations for each chapter.)

Other Books and Resources
from Darrell Johnson:

*Discipleship on the Edge: An Expository Journey
through the Book of Revelation*

Ephesians: The Wonder and Walk of Being Alive in Christ

*Fifty-Seven Words That Change The World:
A Journey Through The Lord's Prayer*

The Beatitudes: Living In Sync With The Reign of God

*Experiencing the Trinity: Living in the Relationship
at the Centre of the Universe*

The Story That Makes Sense Of Our Stories: Genesis 1-11

*The Glory of Preaching: Participating in God's
Transformation of the World*

Find these and other books by Darrell at
DARRELLJOHNSON.CA/BOOKS

———

The Darrell Johnson Podcast

Listen to hundreds of Darrell's sermons from the 1990s
to present day. Available wherever you stream.

DARRELL JOHNSON has been preaching Jesus Christ and His Gospel for over 50 years. He has served a number of Presbyterian congregations in California, Union Church of Manila in the Philippines, and the historic First Baptist Church in the heart of Vancouver, Canada. He has taught preaching for Fuller Theological Seminary, Carey Theological College in Vancouver, and Regent College in Vancouver. He has authored several books, including The Glory of Preaching and Discipleship on the Edge: An Expository Journey Through Revelation.

He is currently serving as a scholar-in-residence at The Way Church Vancouver and the Canadian Church Leaders Network.

He and his wife Sharon have been married for over 50 years. Together they have raised four children adopted from four different countries of the world, and now enjoy loving 11 active grandchildren!

CONTENTS

FOREWORD

BY CHRIS PRICE

You are holding in your hands a book on the Ten Commandments—the most famous law code in the history of the world. Few people today may have memorized the Ten Commandments as the Israelites did, but most people have heard of them. Throughout church history, the Ten Commandments were one of the primary ways pastors and theologians catechized the church, or taught the church Biblical truths. Century after century, the Ten Commandments were required learning for new believers, which is why I think this book ought to be required reading for every follower of Jesus.

The title "Ten Commandments" doesn't appear in the Bible. In scripture it is simply, the ten words.

For those familiar with Genesis chapter one, it is fascinating that ten times in the opening chapter of the Bible we read the refrain, "And God spoke."

God speaks ten times in the original creation.

And, at Sinai, God speaks again—ten words that if followed will form Israel into a renewed creation, a kingdom of priests reflecting the character of Yahweh to the rest of the nations, fulfilling humanity's original vocation. These ten words were crucial in forming Israel's identity as a newly liberated nation, rescued from slavery in Egypt.

But why should *we* study *their* ancient law code?

What benefit is there to following the Ten Commandments today?

Why spend time reading Darrell's book on this subject?

My answer is threefold.

The first two reasons relate to the content of the law code.

The third reason relates to the author of this book.

1. The Role of Rules

We all know every relationship needs rules to flourish. Every roommate situation. Every friendship. And every marriage. Of course, the rules may be unspoken, but they exist nonetheless. We might not discover any particular "rule" until we break it and see the person's reaction, which clearly reveals we have transgressed some type of personal boundary. In the healthiest of relationships, these rules aren't burdensome or unnecessarily restrictive. Rather, the goal is always to bring life and health to the relationship.

The same is true in scripture.

As Jen Wilken writes:

> The Christian faith is absolutely about relationships. But while that faith is personal, it is also communal. We are saved into

a special relationship with God, and thereby into a special relationship with other believers. Christianity is about a relationship with God and others, and because this statement is true, Christianity is also unapologetically about rules, for rules show us how to live in those relationships. *Rather than threaten relationship, rules enable it* [emphasis added].[1]

Darrell argues brilliantly for this perspective on the law of God. As he points out, God's law is never an *imposition* on the human species. Rather, it is an *explanation* of how the human species was created to flourish in community. As such, the Ten Commandments could be looked upon as ten loving invitations toward our own flourishing. What could be more worthy of our study and time?

2. Moving Beyond Moral Relativism

The Ten Commandments are, at a very basic level, a moral code.

An objective, binding moral code, endorsed by the Creator of humanity.

Without God (and without God's endorsement) morality is relative to people, times and places.

As Kevin DeYoung writes, "Can a truly authoritative moral law exist without the existence of a divine law-giver? The obvious answer, according to the Bible, is that it cannot. If our moral obligations are to have any force or binding obligation behind them,

---

1 Jen Wilkin, *Ten Words to Live By* (Wheaton, Ill: Crossway Publishing, 2021), 13.

they must rest on more than majority opinion, or own internal sense of right and wrong, or (heaven forbid) an internet poll."[2]

If God is not the ground, or anchor, for moral values and duties, it means that moral values and duties have to be grounded in, or anchored to, individuals, or cultures—personal preference, or the general populace.

To say it more simply, if there is no God, who makes up morality?

The answer: We do.

What are the logical implications of this answer?

Always some version of moral relativism. What is right for you, might be wrong for me and vice versa.

Morality is like personal taste.

One person likes vanilla.

Another likes chocolate.

One is not actually better than the other. It is simply personal preference.

One doesn't solve the problem by moving beyond the individual to the collective, or by speaking about the greatest amount of good for the greatest number of people, as the utilitarian is prone to do.

After all, one culture's good might be another culture's evil.

And, without God, there is no way to anchor objective morality that should be binding on everyone.

Many atheist thinkers have pointed this out.

Listen to what the atheist, Dr. Alex Rosenberg, a professor

---

2 Kevin DeYoung, *The 10 Commandments: What They Mean, Why They Matter, Why We Should Obey Them* (Wheaton, ILL: Crossway Publishing, 2018), 28.

from Duke University, writes in his book, *The Atheist's Guide to Reality*:

> What is the purpose of the universe? There is none. What is the meaning of life? Ditto. Is there free will? Not a chance. What is the difference between right and wrong, good and bad? There is no moral difference between them. Anything goes.[3]

Friedrich Nietzsche, another famous atheist, pointed out that if God dies so does Christian morality. Objective moral values are vaporized in a universe where God is wiped from the horizon of our lives.

Richard Dawkins, with a touch of rhetorical flourish, writes, "The universe we observe has precisely the properties we should expect if there is, at bottom, no design, no purpose, no evil, no good, nothing but blind, pitiless indifference."[4]

No good.

No evil.

Just indifference.

Machiavelli understood this and concluded that might equals right. Hobbes, Nietzsche, and the great French Existentialists (Sartre, Camus etc), all understood this. Bertrand Russell and the Logical Positivists understood this (after all, given a strict verificationism, moral statements are worse than false, they are meaningless). Michael Foucault believed this and all those postmodernists who still subscribe to truth claims as a masked

---

3 Alex Rosenberg, *The Atheist's Guide to Reality: Enjoying Life without Illusions* (New York: W.W. Norton & Company, 2011), 3.
4 Richard Dawkins, *River Out of Eden* (New York: Basic Books, 1995), 133.

will to power would agree. The great philosophical atheist J.L. Mackie understood this. The prominent philosopher of science Michael Ruse understands this. The utilitarian Peter Singer and his followers understand this. Yuval Harrari, author of the best-seller Sapiens: *A Brief History of Humankind*, argues that once you accept that life evolved by material processes, apart from God's guiding hand, there is no logical basis for human rights.

The list of influential intellectuals goes on and on.

No God, no objective moral values and duties—moral relativism reigns supreme.

The problem is humans can't thrive as moral relativists.

To see why, think of just one chilling example: Is child abuse only wrong in Canada? And not wrong in Russia, or Iraq? Or, is child abuse wrong everywhere? In other words, is it objectively wrong, independent of one's opinion or agreement, for all people in all places? If child abuse is legalized by a culture, is child abuse still wrong, regardless of what the people who made those laws think?

I want to say yes. I assume you do as well. We hope to say yes with the same type of certainty we bring to the conclusion that two plus two equals four. And, if someone doesn't agree with us, we probably don't want them watching our children, or anyone else's for that matter. Yet as soon as we say there are certain actions that are truly wrong and truly right and, therefore, should be binding everywhere, we are no longer acting as a moral relativist and we find ourselves on the horns of a dilemma.

In agreement with many atheistic academics, we should conclude that without the existence of God, we are mired in moral relativism.

But because we cannot consistently live as moral relativists without searing our consciences and amputating a part of our humanity, we are stuck.

That is, until we reintroduce the existence of God as a coherent foundation for objective morality, whether we believe in Him or not.

Philosopher William Lane Craig puts it this way:

1) If God doesn't exist, objective moral values and duties do not exist.

2) Objective moral values and duties do exist.

3) Therefore, God must exist.[5]

The easiest way to "refute" this argument is by misunderstanding it altogether.

So, to be clear, no one should claim you have to believe in God to do good things. Darrell's book refuses to make such a claim. Nor do you need to believe in God to recognize that kindness is better than cruelty. There are plenty of kind atheists to go around. Moreover, genuine moral disagreement will still exist between people who believe in God and read the Bible. After all, moving from agreed upon moral principles to the application of those principles to complex problems can be challenging! There won't always be total consensus. Lastly, we shouldn't conclude that people who believe in God are always better than people who don't. Instead we might even agree with C.S. Lewis—the worst kind of bad man, is a religious bad man.[6]

---

5 William Lane Craig and Walter Sinnott-Armstrong, *God? A Debate between A Christian and an Atheist* (New York NY: Oxford Univ. Press, 2004), 17–21, 67–69.
6 See C.S. Lewis, *Reflections on the Psalms.*

Nevertheless, what we should logically affirm is that even if we don't believe in God, we have to live like God exists.

Every time we condemn an action as really wrong for all people, in all places.

Every time we talk about morality progressing closer to some objective good.

Every time we talk about the way the world "ought" to be, even if those people over there disagree.

Every time we invoke the principle of human rights.

We affirm the necessity of God's existence.

The Ten Commandments make the connection between God and ethics and, in doing so, invite us to live in a coherent moral universe.

As such, they are a gift to the world and worthy of another book unpacking their relevance for our lives.

3. A Fresh Perspective

Darrell Johnson happens to be a brilliant pastor, preacher and practical theologian. These pages are brimming with original insights and profound exegesis and explanation of these famous commandments. The introduction alone is worth the price of this book. For the layperson and the well-read pastor and preacher, Darrell's work will provide many "ah ha" moments. For the person curious about scripture—its power and continued relevance—Darrell's words will also be a helpful guide.

I have taught the Bible for fifteen years, and I have never done an extended study on the Ten Commandments until just recently. I was floored by how much there was to learn, discover and unpack. I found myself agreeing with pastors and theologians throughout church history; the Ten Commandments are critical for followers of Jesus and, I believe, Darrell's work is a significant contribution to the churches' on-going study of the most famous moral code the world has ever known.

For these three reasons, and many others not mentioned, I am thrilled you picked up this book.

PREFACE

Early in the 21st century, when I began thinking about writing this book, a Federal Judge in the United States (in Birmingham, Alabama) was forced by a higher court to remove from the lobby of his courtroom a rock monument on which are carved the Ten Commandments. Whether it was right (i.e. just) in our pluralistic age to force the judge to do it is beyond my expertise to say. What I can say is that, in the final analysis, it does not matter. Why? Because the Ten Commandments, given to Moses thousands of years ago, are carved into the texture of our humanity. Removing the words of the commandments from the public square does not remove them from the fabric of our being.

Imagine a plaque hanging on the wall of a courtroom (or classroom) with the law of gravity (or the law of electro-magnetism) inscribed on it. Imagine that it was ruled that such a plaque was illegal. Does taking it off the wall change anything? Does removing the plaque from the room negate the reality of the law? No. Why? Because the "law" of gravity is constitutive of life in a physical universe.

So too the Ten Commandments. They are ingrained in the way we humans are constituted. When we embrace and function according to these basic "built in" laws we live in alignment with the way it was meant to be.

No one would ever accuse Jesus of Nazareth of being legalistic, of being caught up in rule-making and rule-keeping. Yet, it was He who most affirmed the eternal validity and relevance of the commandments. Near the beginning of His famous Sermon on the Mount He says, "Do not think that I came to abolish the Law or the Prophets; I did not come to abolish, but to fulfill. For truly [literally, 'amen'; Jesus' way of saying 'here is something upon which you can throw all your weight'] I say to you, until heaven and earth pass away, not the smallest letter or stroke shall pass away from the Law, until all is accomplished" (Matthew 5:17-18). For Jesus, the Law with its commandments is as durable as heaven and earth. We can no more remove the Ten Commandments from life than we can remove heaven and earth.

And living in sync with the Ten Commandments leads to life, life as it was designed to be lived. And living in sync with the commandments leads to a life of freedom.

Really? Life and freedom?

Turn the page and see.

EXODUS 20:1–17

Then God spoke all these words, saying,

"I am the LORD your God, who brought you out of the land of Egypt, out of the house of slavery.

"You shall have no other gods before Me.

"You shall not make for yourself an idol, or any likeness of what is in heaven above or on the earth beneath or in the water under the earth. You shall not worship them or serve them; for I, the LORD your God, am a jealous God, visiting the iniquity of the fathers on the children, on the third and the fourth generations of those who hate Me, but showing lovingkindness to thousands, to those who love Me and keep My commandments.

"You shall not take the name of the LORD your God in vain, for the LORD will not leave him unpunished who takes His name in vain.

"Remember the sabbath day, to keep it holy. Six days you shall labor and do all your work, but the seventh day is a sabbath of the LORD your God; *in it* you shall not do any work, you or your son or your daughter, your male or your female servant or your cattle or your sojourner who stays with you. For in six days the LORD made the heavens and the earth, the sea and all that is in them, and rested on the seventh day; therefore the LORD blessed the sabbath day and made it holy.

"Honor your father and your mother, that your days may be prolonged in the land which the LORD your God gives you.

"You shall not murder.

"You shall not commit adultery.

"You shall not steal.

"You shall not bear false witness against your neighbor.

"You shall not covet your neighbor's house; you shall not covet your neighbor's wife or his male servant or his female servant or his ox or his donkey or anything that belongs to your neighbor."

JEALOUS FOR OUR FREEDOM

Here is the context for the words we read in Exodus 20:1-17.

Tens of thousands of people, who fifty days before had been freed from slavery and oppression, were making their way across the Sinai Desert on their way to the Promised Land. They had made camp at the foot of Mt. Sinai.

On that particular day, the mountain slowly became engulfed by smoke, which was pouring from what appeared to be fire on top of the mountain. Lightning flashed in the thick cloud. The sound of trumpets grew louder and louder. The whole mountain began to quake.

The people stood in rapt attention, for they knew that the Living God, the Mighty God, the Holy God had descended upon the mountain. The people trembled in awe. And they feared for their friend and leader Moses. For, while the lightning flashed and the trumpets blasted and the ground shook, Moses was on the mountain! The Liberating God had called him up into that cloud of smoke.

Finally, Moses came down from the mountain. He emerged

from that awesome, terrifying Presence unharmed. Indeed, he glowed! And he had a word from the God whose name is Yahweh. More exactly *he had ten words from Yahweh*. Still more exactly, *Yahweh's ten words had Moses.*

Throughout the Bible, the Ten Commandments—sometimes called The Ten Words (Exodus 34:28)—are celebrated as a gift of God's grace, as a great gift of God's great grace. As Old Testament scholar Gerhard von Rad put it, God, declaring the Ten Commandments, speaking the Ten Words, is celebrated as a saving act of the first order.[1]

So much so that Israel, by God's specific direction, gladly established an annual, weeklong feast to celebrate the giving of the Law. Israel observed three annual feasts: Passover, Tabernacles, and Pentecost. They were as big a deal centuries ago as Christmas, Easter, Mother's Day, and the Fourth of July are in our time. Passover celebrates the exodus—God's liberation of Israel from four hundred years of slavery in Egypt. Tabernacles celebrates the forty years Israel spent wandering in the desert, when God graciously provided water and food, when God graciously guided the people with a cloud by day and a pillar of fire by night, and when the people lived in tents and God graciously dwelt among them in a tent called the tabernacle. Pentecost (the word simply means "the fiftieth," referring to fifty days after Passover) celebrates God's gift of the Law. And the dominant note of that feast is joy!

Imagine that! People celebrating with joy because Someone has interrupted their lives by speaking a new Law.

---

1 Gerhard von Rad, *Old Testament Theology Vol. I*, (Edinburgh: Oliver and Boyd, 1962), 193.

Why? Why would anyone want to celebrate the giving of the Law?

The answer is the thesis of this book. It is a surprising thesis. Especially in our day, when on the one hand the whole idea of right and wrong is being discarded as obsolete, and when on the other hand, as people like Martin Luther King have tried to show us, human law can become the actual oppressor and the enforcer of injustice.

The surprising thesis is this: The Living and Holy God speaks the Ten Commandments in order *to protect and enhance the life of freedom.* The Living and Holy God, who has a name, a personal name, the name "Yahweh" (which is usually translated and obscured by the title "Lord"), and who wants to be called by that name, speaks the Ten Commandments in order to protect and enhance the life of freedom. God had rescued the Hebrew slaves *from,* and had rescued the Hebrew slaves *for: from* bondage and oppression, *for* relationship with Yahweh and with each other. That is how it always is with God: God frees us from, to free us for. God freed them from slavery of all kinds, for relationship, for intimacy and wholeness and trust. From the top of the mountain ablaze with fire, shrouded in smoke, the Living and Holy God declares, "I am Yahweh your God, who brought you out of slavery." And then, from the top of the mountain, He speaks Ten Words in order to protect and enhance the new freedom.

As we read the rest of the Bible, one of the surprising discoveries we make is how closely connected the giving of the Law is with the promise of life.[2] Again and again we hear the claim that in speaking the Law, Yahweh is speaking life:

2 Ibid.

Deuteronomy 4:1: God says, "Now, O Israel, listen to the statutes and the judgments which I am teaching you to perform, in order *that you may live....*"

Deuteronomy 5:29: God says, "Oh that they had such a heart in them, that they would fear Me and keep all My commandments always, *that it may be well with them* and with their children forever!"

Deuteronomy 30:15–16: Moses says, "See, I have set before you today life and good, and death and evil; in that I command you today to love Yahweh your God, to walk in His ways and to keep His commandments...*that you may live.*"

"Love Yahweh; keep His commandments so that you may live." Love. Keep. Jesus also connects the two verbs: "If you love Me, you will keep My commandments (John 14:23).

We see this close connection between Law and life in Psalm 19. The Psalm is composed in two halves. The first half celebrates the goodness of God's Creation; the second celebrates the goodness of God's Law. *Life through Creation:* "The heavens are telling of the glory of God; and their expanse is declaring the work of his Hands" (19:1). *Life through the Law:* "The law of Yahweh is perfect, restoring the soul; ...the precepts of Yahweh are right, rejoicing the heart; the commandments of Yahweh are pure, enlightening the eyes.... They are more desirable than gold, yes, than much fine gold; sweeter also than honey and the drippings of the honeycomb" (19:7–10).

Really? God's commandments are more desirable than gold? They are sweeter than honey?

Why?

Israel celebrates the giving of the Law of Yahweh *because Yahweh gives the Law in order to protect and enhance life, the life of freedom.* It is a surprising thesis.

Let us work with this thesis in three steps. First, defend the thesis. Second, demonstrate the thesis. And third, deal with the problem posed by our apparent inability to live God's Law.

But, before we do any of that, I want to make sure that the whole discussion takes place under an umbrella, the umbrella of the opening line of the Law. If we lose touch with this line, the commandments become a crushing burden and there can be no celebration.

Let me ask you a question: Without looking at your Bible, can you say what the first line of the Law is? Most people answer, "You shall have no other gods before Me." But that is not the first line. It is the first commandment, but it is not the first line. The first line, the opening line, is "I am Yahweh your God.... I am Yahweh your God who brought you out of the house of slavery" (20:2). What is the point? The point is hugely critical: God's commandments are spoken after God's work of redemption. That is, the Law comes after grace. The Law is given in the context of grace. More specifically, Israel is already "saved" when she receives the Law. Which means, keeping the Law is not the means for "getting saved." Israel is already in relationship with God before God speaks the Law. Keeping the Law is, therefore, not the means for winning God's favor. Hallelujah!

In his so-called "letters of freedom"—his letters to the Romans and the Galatians—the Apostle Paul, the "apostle of freedom", as F. F. Bruce calls him,[3] argues that where Israel of old went wrong was separating the commandments, "Thou

---

3 F.F. Bruce, *Paul: Apostle of the Heart Set Free* (Grand Rapids: Eerdmans, 1977).

shall not" from the prologue, "I am Yahweh your God who has redeemed you." Israel, and much of the Church after her, thereby changed a gift of grace into a means to get grace. But the Exodus text is crystal clear: the Law comes after grace, as a gift of grace, given to protect and enhance a life of grace.[4]

Some people seem to think that the first line of the Law is this: "Keep these commandments and then I will free you; keep these commandments and then I will love you." No! A thousand times no! The first line of the Law can be paraphrased, "I am Yahweh your God, I already love you, I have already acted to free you." God then speaks the commandments *to protect and enhance the life of freedom given to us by grace.*

1. Let us now defend this surprising thesis.

There are two basic lines of defense: the first is sociological; the second is theological.

(A) THE SOCIOLOGICAL DEFENSE

After the exodus from Egypt, the pressing issue became how to live together on a daily basis. It is the pressing issue after any revolution: "Now what?" "How do we make it work?" For years the people had lived in slavery. What does it mean for us to now live in freedom? It was the question after the People Power Revolution in the Philippines in 1986. Now that the dictator is gone, how do we make it work?[5]

---

4 See Romans 9:30–3.
5 My family and I were living in the Philippines at that time, I served as the Pastor of the Union Church of Manila.

Out in the desert, Israel has two options. Either Moses can continue as the absolute leader-ruler, or the community can simply evolve around natural power centers.[6] The first option leads to a dictatorship, the second to anarchy. The first option (dictatorship) fails because there is no protection of the ruled against the rulers. The second option (anarchy) fails because there are no clear boundaries, no common ground for dialogue and cooperation, and, therefore, there is no security.

Out in the Sinai desert, the Living God gives Israel—and all peoples—a third option, a way between the two extremes of dictatorship and anarchy. In place of any human authority, God speaks the Divine Law. My friend Earl Palmer puts it this way: Moses goes up Mt. Sinai as the absolute ruler of the people; he comes down from Mt. Sinai set free from his own absoluteness. He comes down himself a person under a higher authority.[7]

It is significant to note that, after receiving the Law, there is a new boldness in Moses. Why? Moses had a new boldness because he now stood upon and stood under a higher authority than himself. Now he could say, "Thus says the Lord."

The gift of the Law also sets the lowest citizen free. From now on the "average Israelite" has a place from which to challenge the most powerful of leaders. The "average Israelite" could now walk into Moses' tent and also say, "Thus says the Lord." The gift of Law frees the ruler and the ruled.[8] Where there is a common standard of right and wrong, there is great freedom.

---

6 Earl Palmer helped me see this in a sermon he preached at College Briefing Conference at Forest Home Christian Conference Center (Southern California) in 1972.

7 Ibid.

8 Ibid.

Which explains the paralysis of the so-called "free world." There is no such common ground. *The Washington Post* laments, "Common decency can no longer be called common."[9] Richard Neuhaus is right: We are a society with "a naked public square."[10] We have no standard by which to say right is right and wrong is wrong. We have no moral center. All transcendent values have been removed.

History has shown that the rule of relativism only and always leads to confusion. When there is no rulebook how do you know how to play the game?

"Rejoice," says Moses. The Living God wants us to play with gusto. So God has given us the rulebook!

But why *this* rulebook? Why *these* particular commandments? Why not another set of commandments?

We come to the second line of defense of this surprising thesis.

(B) THE THEOLOGICAL DEFENSE

Yahweh's commandments protect and enhance freedom because they "fit the species." Which explains why, until recently, they have held such a central place in Western civilization. Even those who did not affirm their Divine origin still held Yahweh's Ten Words in high regard. There is something about them that "fits" us human beings.

Why? For this one simple reason: Yahweh knows what makes us tick. The Lawgiver is not only the Redeemer; the Lawgiver is also the Creator. This is critical to realize and affirm. The Giver

---

9 In a 1979 editorial.
10 See his excellent book with that title.

of the Law is the One who made us. Yahweh drew up the blue-prints for the human species. Yahweh is the One who designed us magnificently complex creatures. And in Yahweh's Law, we are given "The Manufacturer's Specifications" As they say, "When all else fails, read the owner's manual." In the Ten Commandments, the Creator and Owner tells us how we humans best function in the created order.

You can see then, that to ignore or go against Yahweh's Law is to go against the grain of our essential nature. When we violate Yahweh's good Law, we violate reality. We violate ourselves.

This is clearly the case with the sixth commandment, "You shall not murder." But it is also the case with the ninth commandment, "You shall not bear false witness." Twisting the facts always complicates life, constricting movement, draining life of vitality.

So, too, with the fourth commandment: "Six days you shall labor and do all your work, but the seventh day is a Sabbath to Yahweh your God. On it you shall not do any work." The Living God is not imposing some arbitrary rule upon life. Nor is God simply giving "friendly advice to weary people." The Living One is *telling us a mystery*. The Creator is telling us something essential about ourselves: that human beings are sabbatically constituted—"six plus one" is stamped upon the very fabric of our being. In the commandment, God is saying, "This is who you are: you were made in such a way that you operate most *effectively*, most humanely, on the sabbatical rhythm—six plus one."

The same thing is true with the seventh commandment, "You shall not commit adultery." God is not imposing some arbitrary rule upon life; God does not want to squelch joy. The Living One is *telling us a mystery about our humanity*. The mystery is that we were made for fidelity; hopping in and out of bed with many sex partners violates *who we are.*

Yahweh's Law protects and enhances because it "fits" the species. E. Stanley Jones put it this way: the Law is not an "imposition" on the human species; it is an "exposition" of how the human species was created to live.[11] That is why John can say in his first letter, "His commandments are not burdensome" (1 John 5:3)." They tell us who we were created to be.

This line of defense goes even deeper. For Yahweh did not, so to speak, spin the Law out of thin air. The commandments emerge out of Yahweh's nature and character. The commandments reveal Yahweh's nature and character. In the Law, the Living God is painting a Self-portrait. "You shall not bear false witness." Why? "Because I, your God, will not. I am utterly reliable. I mean what I say and say what I mean." "You shall not commit adultery." Why? "Because I, your God, will not. I am utterly faithful. I keep My commitments; I protect My relationships."

This conviction that in the Law the Lawgiver is revealing His character is built into the Hebrew word translated "Law". It is the word *torah*. The noun comes from the word which means "to shoot, to throw, to teach," and thus, "to reveal." "When one man teaches another, he shoots ideas from his own into the others' mind. But in so doing he 'reveals' what is on his own."[12] When Yahweh "threw" His commandments to us, He "shot" ideas from His own mind and heart into our minds and hearts, thereby revealing His own heart and mind. This is why in Psalms 1, 19, and 119, the Psalmist speaks of "loving" the Law. Loving the Law? Is he nuts? No. The Psalmist loves the Torah because

---

11 In his book on Jesus' Sermon on the Mount, *The Christ of the Mount.*
12 George Knight, quoted by Eugene Peterson, *Answering God.*

in it and through it the torah-ing One has made Himself known. The Psalmist loves the Giver of the Law. (The ultimate, final Torah is Jesus Christ, God speaking for Himself in person; see John 1:1-18.)

Yahweh's Law is no "alien ethic." It emerges from who God is and therefore, like God, is eternally contemporary, eternally relevant. When Yahweh came to us as one of us, as Jesus of Nazareth, He said in His Sermon on the Mount, "Do not think that I came to abolish the Law...I did not come to abolish, but to fulfill. For truly I say to you, until heaven and earth pass away, not the smallest letter or stroke shall pass away from the Law, until all is accomplished" (Matthew 5:17–18). The Law of God is as enduring as the Universe of God and as enduring as the character of God.

God's Law protects and enhances the life of freedom, first because it makes for order, and second because it reveals the structure of reality, *telling us who God is and who God made us to be*. To neglect or to transgress the good Law of the good God is to buck reality. We are most free when we live by Yahweh's Ten Words.

2. Let us now demonstrate the thesis.

The first three commandments protect and enhance *relationship with the Living God*.

"You shall have no other gods before Me.
"You shall not make for yourself an idol...
"You shall not take the name of Yahweh your God in vain..."

Exodus 20:3–7

27

These three commandments free us by warning us of our capacity for idolatry. Idolatry always destroys life, for we were not only made by the Living God, we were made for the Living God. If we allow any other god, or god-substitute, however good, to come between us and the Living God, we are going to lose. Yahweh alone can fulfill our deepest longings. For our sakes, Yahweh calls for exclusive allegiance. "I am the jealous God," the God who passionately desires relationship and will tolerate no false lovers. And for our sakes, God forbids making any likeness of the Divine for, in the words of Alan Cole, "no likeness could possibly be adequate, and...each type of image would imprint its own misunderstanding" of God on our hearts.[13] God wants to be known as God really is. To summarize the profound insights of Joy Davidman in her work on the second commandment, "The first three commandments free us from little gods for the One, True, Living God."[14]

The fourth commandment, as already noted, protects and enhances *a balanced life*. "Remember the Sabbath day to keep it holy." Here God sets us free from "rat-race-ness" for "human-race-ness." Freedom, not to mention effectiveness, is found in the six-plus-one rhythm. I believe that much of the neurosis and sickness in modern life is fundamentally due to ignoring God's good law and I believe much sanity and wholeness would return if we obeyed.

Commandments five through ten protect and enhance our *relationship with the community*. God begins with the relationship

---

13 Alan Cole, *Exodus: An Introduction and Commentary* (Downers Grove, Illinois: Inter-Varsity Press, 1973), 155.
14 Joy Davidman, *Smoke on the Mountain: An Interpretation of the Ten Commandments* (Philadelphia: Westminster Press, 1954), 30-39.

closest to us, with parents. Commandment five: "Honor your father and your mother." "Honor" means more than "obey." It means to highly prize (Proverbs 4:8), to show respect for, to take care of. The fifth commandment is given to protect us in our old age, to safeguard a place for the aged within the community.

Commandment six, "You shall not murder," safeguards our neighbor's physical life. Commandment seven, "You shall not commit adultery," safeguards our neighbor's marriage. Commandment eight, "You shall not steal," safeguards our neighbor's property. Commandment nine, "You shall not bear false witness," safeguards our neighbor's reputation.

Oh, how foolish we are to throw away God's good words! Once we play around with these commandments, the fabric of community begins to unravel. And there is a return to bondage. No wonder the Psalmist cries the way he does in Psalm 119:136: "My eyes shed streams of water, because they do not keep Your Law." How he would have cried in our day when day after day, night after night, on our public media, adultery and murder are glorified. How he would cry in our day when little ones and old people are thought of as "in the way," virtually treated as non-persons.

The key commandment that protects and enhances the life of freedom is the tenth: "You shall not covet your neighbor's house; you shall not covet your neighbor's wife or his male servant or his female servant or his ox or his donkey [or his new Lexus] or anything that belongs to your neighbor." Here God frees us from ourselves. God frees us by warning us about our hearts, telling us that our hearts have a tendency to crave what is not our own. That is putting it mildly! Here God calls us to examine and check the unspoken desires and yearnings. For if I crave my neighbor's spouse long enough, the desire gives birth to fantasizing, which one day leads to action. If I crave my neighbor's status long enough, the desire can move me either to usurp her position by force, or whittle her down by spreading rumors. The Loving God wants us to live! So He protects us against our sin while it is still inside.

Now, the fact is, breaking the tenth commandment is a sign, the clearest sign, that we have broken the first commandment—that we are, at that particular moment of craving what is not our own, living for another god. For the sign that we are living in exclusive allegiance to Yahweh is contentment—contentment with Yahweh's love for us. "Yahweh is my shepherd, I shall not want" (Psalm 23:1).

3. We are now ready for the third step in our study: dealing with the problem posed by our apparent inability to live God's good law.

If God's Law is describing the freedom life, if God's Law reveals who God is and who God made us to be, and if we keep failing to live up to it, then we are in an awful bind. Is there a way out?

Yes! Yahweh to the rescue! Jesus. In Hebrew, *Y'shua*, meaning Yahweh-to-the-Rescue. The Lawgiver comes down from the top of the mountain, all the way down, and becomes one of us. And as one of us, "born under the Law" (Galatians 4:5), Jesus frees us to live the life of freedom. How? Not by discarding the Law and not by watering it down to make it fit our sinful condition. That is the error of liberalism. Not by rubbing our face in the Law; not by banging the Law over our heads. That is the error of fundamentalism. Instead, Jesus—Yahweh-to-the-Rescue—*does two unexpected and amazing things.*

First, He forgives us! He forgives those who are sorry for their transgressions and rebellion. The Author of the Law pardons the repentant law-breakers! "Amazing grace, how sweet the sound." The Apostle Paul puts it most vividly in his letter to the Colossians: "Christ has utterly wiped out the damning evidence of broken laws and commandments which always hung over our heads, and has completely annulled it by nailing it over His head on the cross" (Colossians 2:14, J. B. Phillips). The Lawgiver comes down from the mountain, enters the valley of transgressions and rebellion, and then climbs another mountain. On that mountain, on Calvary, the Lawgiver takes upon Himself the judgment we law-breakers deserve. Through that act, He restores the broken relationship and relieves the crippling guilt. Yahweh-to-the-rescue heals the awful breach in reality.

Then He does a second thing. He empowers us to obey. He empowers us to live "The Manufacturer's Specifications." The two actions always go together: forgiveness and empowerment.

As a human being, Jesus Christ perfectly lives the good Law. "Yes," we say, "but He had an advantage. He was the Son of God—God the Son." True. The very life of God dwelt in Him, enabling Him to live consistent with the blueprint. But what does the Gospel say? What happens to people whom He calls into relationship, into discipleship? *Does He not transfer the "advantage" to them? To us?* Yes! Yahweh-to-the Rescue breathes His Spirit into us, granting us His supernatural power to live the life of freedom.

Again the Apostle Paul puts it so well: "For what the Law could not do, weak as it was through the flesh, God did: sending His own Son in the likeness of sinful flesh and as an offering for sin, He condemned sin in the flesh, in order that the requirement of the Law might be fulfilled in us, who do not walk by the power of the flesh, but by the power of the Spirit" (Romans 8:3-4). (I take Paul's "according to" in 8:4 to mean "by the power of.") Jesus Christ overcomes the problem posed by our inability. He suffers on the cross and sends the Spirit. He forgives us and empowers us.

I noted at the beginning of the introductory chapter that Israel celebrated the giving of the Law at the Feast of Pentecost. Is it mere coincidence that Jesus Christ poured out His Spirit on the Church at Pentecost? It was no coincidence at all! For the Spirit of Yahweh comes to enable the people of Yahweh to live Yahweh's design for human life.

On the day when God spoke from the mountaintop, engulfed in flame and smoke, the people were told to write God's Ten Words on their wrist bands and on a band that dangled in front of their eyes. So jealous was God for their freedom that God also told them to write the commandments on the doorposts of their homes and on the gates in front of their homes. Supposedly, seeing the Law before them, in all of their comings and goings, would issue in obedience. That helped. But only for a while. For the problem was the heart. The problem still is the heart.

So, God promises a new covenant, a new arrangement. Centuries after the mountain-top encounter, God says through the prophet Jeremiah: "Behold, days are coming when I will make a new covenant...not like the covenant which I made with their ancestors in the day I took them by the hand to bring them out of the land of Egypt, My covenant which they broke, although I was a husband to them. But this is the covenant which I will make with them after those days. I will put My Law within them, and on their heart I will write it" (Jeremiah 31:31–33).

That is what the Spirit of Yahweh comes to do. He comes to do heart surgery, not to put a pacemaker into our hearts, but to put the good Law in our hearts. The Holy Spirit comes to make us into "new covenant" people. Taking God's "freedom law" off the tablets of stone, off the doorposts, off the courtroom and schoolroom walls, off the wristbands, and engraving them on the flesh of our hearts.

In light of all of this, I think you can see that in the final analysis, God's commandments turn out to be God's promises. This is because God's Word not only informs, it performs. God's Word brings into being what it announces. "Let there be light!" And there was ... lots of it! And because of what God does for us in the sending of His Son and Spirit, the Ten Commandments turn out to be the Ten Promises.

"I am Yahweh your God,

Who made you

And who became one of you,

And who went to the cross to free you from the consequences
of your rebellious heart.

And I am Yahweh your God,

Who comes to live with you and in you through My Spirit.

"Therefore, because I am Who I am,

And have done for you what I have done for you,

One day you will no longer buck up against the grain of
reality.

One day you will have no other gods before Me; there will be
nothing between us!

You will have no distorted ideas or images of Who I am; you
will know Me as I truly am.

You will not use My Name in vain; You will call upon Me in
every situation and find that I will come to you.

You will live a holy, sabbatically-balanced life; you will know
true rest.

You will honor your mother and father; it will go well for you
in the land.

You will not murder.

You will not commit adultery.

You will not steal.

You will not bear false witness.

And one day you will not covet. You will be satisfied in and
with Me.

"And one day you will love me with all of your heart and soul
and mind and strength.

"And you will love your neighbor as yourself.

And one day you will love one another as I have loved you."

Make it so Lord, for your glory. Make it so.

EXODUS 20:3

"You shall have no other gods before Me."

NO OTHER GODS:
YOU WERE MADE FOR ME ALONE

Before jumping into the first commandment I invite you to take a quiz. Please take out a piece of paper and write down in a column the numbers one to ten. Then please write down next to the numbers, in order, the Ten Commandments. See if you can do it in less than two minutes.

One of the surprising facts of Biblical history, surprising to us in this "antinomian age" (this anti-law age), is that nearly every great renewal movement, nearly every great spiritual revival, was caused, on the human level, by a re-discovery of the commandments, a re-discovery of the Law. Someone, a prophet or priest, finds a copy of the Law, reads it and is stunned into repentance and stirred into joy. The person then brings the copy of the Law to the king and his advisors who read the Law—the commandments—and they are stunned into repentance and stirred into joy. The king then calls for a national assembly where the Law is read out loud and the people are stunned into repentance and stirred into joy. Amazing! It happened during the days of Josiah[1] and Hezekiah and Ezra and Nehemiah.[2] Why?

Why would the reading and hearing of commandments generate a surge of new life?

Because the Author of the commandments, the God whose name is Yahweh, spoke the commandments to protect and enhance a life of freedom. Yahweh had freed nearly three million Hebrew slaves from bondage and oppression, for a relationship with Yahweh and with each other. Yahweh spoke the Ten Commandments or the Ten Words, to protect and enhance that freedom.

Why does Yahweh's Law accomplish this end?

Because the God whose name is Yahweh is the Creator of all things. The Ten Commandments emerge from the Creator's nature and character. The commandments reveal who the Creator is! And the commandments reveal who we are. The commandments tell us who Yahweh created us to be. In the Ten Commandments, we have "The Manufacturer's Specifications." As Old Testament scholar, Terrence E. Fretheim, puts it, "To obey these commandments is to be what one was created to be."[3]

Without doubt, the most critical of the Ten Commandments is the first: "You shall have no other gods before Me." Get this one straight and all the others fall in line. "You shall have no other gods before Me."

You who learned the commandments in the Roman Catholic or Lutheran traditions are surprised that, having said the first

---

1 2 Kings 22:18ff; 2 Chronicles 34:15ff.
2 Nehemiah 7-9.
3 Terence E. Fretheim, *Exodus: Interpretation, A Bible Commentary for Teaching and Preaching* (Louisville: John Knox Press, 1991) 223.

commandment is the most critical, I stopped at the end of "You shall have no other gods before Me." For the Roman Catholic and Lutheran traditions add to those words the words, "You shall not make for yourself an idol," the words the Reformed tradition calls the second commandment. So that in the Roman Catholic and Lutheran traditions, the first commandment is "You shall have no other gods before Me. You shall not make for yourself an idol; you shall not worship them or serve them; for I, Yahweh your God, am a jealous God."

The reason for the difference is that, whereas the Bible says there are Ten Commandments, or ten words (Exodus 34:28; Deuteronomy 4:13; 10:4), the Bible does not number them. Nowhere do we find, "This is number one, this is number two; this is number five; this is number nine." Thus different traditions number and divide the commandments differently. The Reformed tradition, along with the Eastern Orthodox and Armenian Orthodox traditions, separate having no other gods before God from not making images and idols, counting them as numbers one and two. Roman Catholics and Lutherans having combined them as the first commandment, then separate the words about coveting into two distinct commandments: number nine, "You shall not covet your neighbor's house," and number ten, "You shall not covet your neighbor's wife or his male servant or his female servant...," etc. Our Jewish friends break the commandments down into yet another configuration. They take the opening line, the prologue, "I am Yahweh your God..." as the first "word." They combine the Reformed tradition's one and two to form the second "word." They keep the two statements about coveting as the tenth "word."

Clearly commandments one and two, as they are numbered by the Reformed tradition, are closely related. They belong together. For one thing, they both address the same issue—our relationship with the Living God. For another, they are both theologically grounded in the same dimension of God's character—in Yahweh's jealousy. They both pose the fundamental issue of our lives: for whom will I live; whom will I serve; whom will I worship?

In the first two commandments (as in the other eight), the Creator is telling us something fundamental about ourselves, something deeply ingrained in our essential being. In these first two commandments the Creator is telling us that we are *worshiping* creatures. Birds fly in the air. Fish swim in the sea. Cats meow. Dogs bark. And human beings worship. Which explains why we cannot live without a hero. We are created to adore and trust something or someone. It is in our genes. Everyone has a god that she or he adores and trusts. It may not be a personal God like the One who comes to us in the exodus, in the Law, in the prophets, and finally in and as Jesus of Nazareth. But everyone lives for some god, for something or someone of ultimate concern. It may only be oneself, but everyone adores and trusts some god. As the saying goes, "He is a self-made man who worships his creator."

We cannot escape this fundamental fact about ourselves. No one can "jump out of her or his skin."[4] We are the creatures who worship. Indeed, every act throughout the day is an act of worship of someone or something.

To keep us from ruining our lives, the Living and Holy God,

---

4 As E. Stanley Jones said so often throughout his writings.

out of great mercy and grace, speaks the first two commandments. God warns us of our propensity toward idolatry, toward adoring and trusting what is finally not God.

"You shall have no other gods before Me."

By itself, the first commandment is not teaching us that there is only one God. The Bible clearly teaches that there is only one Yahweh: the Trinitarian God—Father, Son, and Holy Spirit. But that is not the burden of the first commandment. The burden of the first commandment is allegiance. God confronts us with the question "not of theology, but of loyalty."[5] In other parts of Scripture, we do find Yahweh claiming to be the one and only God. In Isaiah, for instance, "I am the first and I am the last, and there is no God besides Me" (Isaiah 44:6); "Is there any God besides Me, or is there any other Rock? I know of none" (Isaiah 44:8) (see also Isaiah 45:6, 14, 21; 46:9; Psalm 62:5–8). But here, in the Law, God does not say, "There are no other gods for you to serve." God says, "You shall have no other gods before Me." The issue is not *monotheism*, belief in one God. The issue is *monolatry*, exclusive allegiance to the one God.

"No other gods before Me." "Before Me." Literally, "In My Presence." "You shall have no other gods in My Presence." And where is God's Presence? Everywhere! "Where can I go from Your Spirit? Or where can I flee from Your Presence?"(Psalm 139:7). The Living God is present everywhere. "You shall have no other gods before Me anywhere, anytime. You shall not let anyone or anything come between you and Me anywhere, anytime. You shall not let anyone or anything take My place in your life, anywhere, anytime."

---

5 J. I. Packer, *Knowing God* (Downers Grove: Inter-Varsity Press, 1973) 243.

Let us dig deeper by asking four questions of the first commandment:

1. Why does God give this commandment?
2. What happens when we do not obey it?
3. How do we obey it?
4. What is the Living God supposed to do when we disobey, which we do more than we care to know?

1. First question: *Why does God give us this commandment, "You shall have no other gods before Me"?*

I ask the question because of the conviction that, if we know why God commands something, we are more likely to be willing to obey. Is that not the case with human laws? If we know why our government has made a certain law, we are more likely to be willing to cooperate...or rise up in protest! Why does the One True God command, "You shall have no other gods before Me"? Because God is lonely and because we are not giving God enough attention? Because God is afraid? Because God is insecure? Because God is mean? Because God is an egotist, a narcissist, who constantly needs praise to feel good about God's self? No!

Why then command us, "You shall have no other gods before Me"? *Because God is telling us something about ourselves we would never have figured out on our own.* The Manufacturer is telling us that we were made in such a way that *only* the Living God can satisfy the longings of our hearts. We were not only made *by* God; we were made *for* God.

In the first commandment, God is paying us an incredible compliment. Really? Yes! God is saying that we are so wonderfully made that only the infinite, holy, all-knowing, all-powerful, ever-present, wise, just, merciful, gracious, eternal God can fill us and fulfill us.

This explains why God says in the Law, "I, Yahweh your God, am a jealous God" (Exodus 20:5). A jealous God. Really? Not in the sense we ordinarily use the word; not as a possessive, insecure, easily threatened lover. Rather, God's jealousy is God's holy zeal to protect something supremely precious.[6] "I am the God who is zealous to protect something supremely precious."

We were made *for* the Living God. What dignity! We were made for a love relationship with the Triune God. We were made to enter into and enjoy the love relationship that has forever thrived between the Father and Son and Holy Spirit. God our passionate lover; we are God's bride. We are called to an exclusive personal relationship. We are to let no other lover take God's place. The good news is that *God will not tolerate other lovers, however loving and loveable they are, coming between God and us.* For God knows that all other lovers, however loving or loveable, cannot finally satisfy the longings of our hearts. All other lovers finally leave us unfulfilled. We were made in such a way that only the infinite God can satisfy our finite hearts.

2. Second question: *What happens when we disobey the first commandment?*

We lose! Simple as that. We end up living for lesser gods, false gods, who all turn out, in the final analysis, to be non-gods. And

---

6 J. I. Packer, Ibid.; Leon Morris, *The Apostolic Preaching of the Cross* (Eerdmans; 1st Edition, 1955).

we spend our lives trying to milk the non-gods for what they finally cannot deliver.

Again, we are the creatures who worship. We worship all of the time. We worship someone or something. It is either the Living God, or someone or something else. But no someone or something else can bear the weight of our human desire for worship. And we either end up being disappointed in the someone or something else, or the someone or something else ends up being drained and destroyed by our making the person or thing into the substitute God.

Furthermore, when we disobey the first commandment, we find ourselves breaking one or all of the other nine. When we let someone or something else come between us and the One, True, and Living God, we soon break the second commandment; we no longer know God as God really is, and start making images of God; we start creating God in our image. We usually end up breaking the third commandment, and use God's name in vain. We will most certainly break the fourth commandment, and no longer choose to keep the Sabbath holy. We will waffle on the fifth, and not honor our mothers and fathers as we ought. Because the non-god, which we have let come between us and the real God, cannot meet the horrendous need of our hearts, we will be tempted to use violence to get what we want, breaking the sixth commandment. We will be tempted to nurture and act on our lusts, breaking the seventh commandment. We will be tempted to take what is not our own, breaking the eighth commandment. We will be tempted to put down those who threaten us, breaking the ninth commandment. And since the non-god who has taken the real God's place cannot fulfill the desires of our hearts, we will break the tenth commandment and anxiously covet everything else but intimacy with God.

Worst of all, when we break the first commandment, we fall into slavery to the non-gods. We end up addicted to things beneath our created dignity.

Oh, God have mercy! Liberator, come and free us again for Yourself!

3. Third question: *How do we obey the first commandment?*

Once we have disobeyed, can we re-obey? Is obedience even possible? Not apart from *grace*.

How then, by grace, do we obey?

By admitting and owning the fact that we do not obey. By admitting and owning our bent toward idolatry. By admitting and owning the fact that we take what are not gods—our spouse, our children, our jobs, our possessions, our technology, our money—and put them in the place only God can occupy.

We obey by affirming that the Living God is in every circumstance, in every situation, present in every encounter with other people. We obey by seeking to see and hear and respond to God in every circumstance and encounter.

We obey by asking ourselves, on a regular basis, tough questions. Here are some of the questions I try to regularly ask myself:

"What is it that gives me a sense of security?" When I look out on the future, what do I instinctively look to as my security, or my family's security? I have to confess that often it is the financial resources that I have saved. We will be fine because of the condo and the modest bank account and the old age income from the government. Can you relate? Those answers are potential God-substitutes. In and of themselves they are good. Indeed, they are good gifts of the God Who wants nothing between me and Him. But those gifts can slowly enter that space only Yahweh has the right to occupy. You may have noticed how that can be the case for me in the way I put it above: "financial resources I have saved." I? I have saved? Well, on one level, yes. But was it not He Who gave me work and provided for me and my family all along? When I think all this through more carefully, I come again to realize that there really is only one final security: the Living God Who brought me into this world, called me into relationship, will take me (and my family) all the way through the journey. With nothing between me and Him I need not be worried about the future.

"What do I fear?" Fear is always a good clue to one's idol. Primitive idols were often projections of what people feared. They would do anything to appease what they feared, so that the thing they feared would do no further harm. What do you fear? Losing money? Then money may be your idol. Rejection? So much so that you will deny your allegiance to Jesus Christ to be welcomed by the group? Then acceptance may be your idol. Loss of health? Then being healthy—a good thing in and of itself—is a potential God-substitute. Clearly so for many in this death-denying culture. Do you fear death? So much so that you are willing to join our death-denying culture in its futile quest for everlasting youth? Then life may be your idol. Life? Yes, life. Even life can become a God-substitute. Even the desire for life (usually on our own terms) can come between us and God. "What do I fear?"

Another question: "What gives me comfort when I am distressed?" To what do I turn when my soul is troubled? Food? Alcohol? Binge movie watching? Or to more destructive comfort-promisers? That only makes things worse?

Another question: "What do I love more than anything else?" The answer is a potential idol. The thing, the activity, the person, may be very good. Indeed, it has to be good or I would not love it. It may even be something God very much wants me to have. But it must not, for my sake, and for its sake, stand or sit in the place where God, and God alone, deserves and desires to sit.

Another question to ask: "So who does the saving anyway?" Who saves us? Who fixes me and the rest of humanity? Technology? I am grateful for so much of it, like the computer on which I am writing. Education? Not a bad thing to have. Prosperity? The church? The pastors? "Who does the saving?" The answer can lead to a potential God-substitute.

One more question. Initially disturbing, so be ready. "What is it in my life, which if God took it away, I would turn from God?" A house? A career? A child? A spouse? Let me put the question more provocatively, and perhaps for some, more painfully. "What is it in my life, which if God took it away, I would hate God?" Sit with the question for a while, and see if it leads you to a God-substitute of which you were not aware.

When we spot a God-substitute, what are we supposed to do? We are to deal with it. We must deal with it. We must move it out of its wrongful place, and into the rightful place. We must move it, or him or her, out of the center. Must? Yes.

For, the fact is, we tend to relate to the Living God through the lens of our commitment to our idol. That is, I will relate to the true God only to the degree that the true God is good for my idol. I will, for instance, not allow myself to see other aspects of the true God if those aspects get in the way of serving my idol. If financial security is my real god, I will have to turn off God's clear call to share my wealth with the poor. If being a well-liked preacher is my real god, I will have to avoid teaching truths about God that people do not like to hear. Anytime you or I have to turn off Biblical truths about God, or have to disobey God's word to keep our relationship with something or someone we love, that someone or something has become a "god before God."

4. Which brings us to the fourth question: *What is God supposed to do when we disobey the first commandment?*

When Yahweh sees us living for or around another god, what is Yahweh supposed to do? God knows that the other god, however good, will ultimately let us down. So what is God supposed to do?

God can warn us that we are on the road to idolatry. God can woo us back. Both of which God does again and again. Mercy!

But when we do not heed the warning or respond to the wooing, what is God supposed to do? *Remove the idol!* God moves the idol out of its wrongful place and puts it back in its rightful place.

God must move it out for our soul's sake. For one day that "god" will not be there. And the pain could be unbearable. And more importantly, before that day that "god" will go sour on us. Why? Because no God-substitute can finally satisfy our souls. Only the Living God Who comes to us in and as Jesus can fill the deep ache in the center of our souls. And God must move the idol out of its wrongful place for its sake. No thing, no person, can bear the weight of our trying to fill our souls with it and her or him. I have prayed with many persons whose parents treated them as God-substituted, and it almost killed them; it certainly drained them. I have walked with many whose spouses put unhuman pressure on them to deliver what only Yahweh can deliver. For our sake, for the God-substitute's sake, God in His mercy moves it out of where it/they do not belong.

(If you want to dig deeper on this I recommend the love story, written by Sheldon Vanauken, who became a friend of C. S. Lewis. It is entitled, *A Severe Mercy.*[7])

You may be thinking that God moving idols is too severe. But I will tell you of something even more severe. It is when God no longer cares that we go after other gods. When God leaves us *alone* with our other gods. The more severe thing the Living God can do is to let us go on living with the *wrong* god at the center (Hosea 4:17). *That* would be *severe judgment.* For we were made for God—to enjoy life, to be fully human, when God, and God alone, lives at the center. We were so wonderfully made that we will *never* be satisfied with anything *less than* God.

"You shall have no other gods before Me."

It is the first commandment.

But because the Law-giver is the passionately zealous lover of our souls, it is also the first *promise*: "You will have no other gods before Me...one day you *will* have no other gods before Me."

---

7 Sheldon Vanauken, *A Severe Mercy* (San Francisco: Harper & Row, 1977).

EXODUS 20:4-6

"You shall not make for yourself an idol or any likeness of what is in heaven above or on the earth beneath or in the water under the earth. You shall not worship them or serve them; for I, Yahweh your God, am a jealous God, visiting the iniquity of the fathers on the children, on the third and the fourth generations of those who hate Me, but showing loving kindness to thousands, to those who love Me and keep My commandments."

DON'T BOX ME IN:
ONLY I CAN TELL YOU WHO I AM

Why does the Living God speak this second commandment?

We have been arguing that God, whose name is Yahweh, spoke all the commandments to protect and enhance a life of freedom. Yahweh had freed three million Hebrew slaves *from* and *for*: *from* bondage and oppression, *for* relationship with Yahweh and with each other. God spoke the Ten Commandments to protect that new freedom and to enhance that new freedom.

How does the second commandment achieve that end?

The second commandment clearly belongs with the first commandment: "You shall have no other gods before Me." Indeed, some Christians, as we have noted, combine the first and second commandments into one.

Why does God speak the second commandment?

Well, why did God speak the first commandment? God speaks the first commandment to keep us from ruining our lives. In the first commandment, God is telling us something about ourselves that we would have never figured out on our own. God is telling us that we were created in such a way that only God can finally satisfy the longings of our hearts. We were not only made *by* God. We were made *for* God. Glory! We were created in such a way that only the Infinite, Holy, all-powerful, all-wise, ever-present, merciful, personal God can fill and fulfill our finite hearts. God speaks the first commandment to keep us from ruining our lives by letting anyone or anything come between us and God. "You shall have no other gods before me."

The second commandment naturally follows: "You shall not make for yourself an idol, or any likeness...." God is telling us that we not only ruin our lives by worshiping the wrong god. We also ruin our lives by worshiping the right God in a wrong way. God is telling us in the first commandment that we are the creature who worships. Birds fly in the sky, fish swim in the sea, cats meow, dogs bark, snakes slither on the ground, and human beings worship, all the time, someone or something. God is telling us in the second commandment that *we are the creature who imagines.* It is part of what it means to be created in God's image: we were created with the capacity to imagine. But because we are, since the fall of Adam and Eve, no longer consistently what we were created to be, our imagining can lead us astray, especially about God. John Calvin, the great Reformer, called us humans, "idol factories." We are always coming up with gods of our own imagining, gods made in our image. In the second commandment God is telling us that *idolatry consists not only in worshiping false gods, but in worshiping the true god in a false way*—using human-made images and likenesses of God.

The first and second commandments are both grounded in the same dimension of God's character: "I, Yahweh your God, am a jealous God...." (Exodus 20:5). This is not the only place in the

Bible where God speaks this way. Later in the book of Exodus, for instance, Exodus 34:14, God says, "...for you shall not worship any other god, for Yahweh, whose name is Jealous, is a jealous God." God's "jealousy" is not "a passing mood, but belongs to the very essence of God."[1]

What does this mean? J. I. Packer asks: "How can jealousy be a virtue in God when it is a vice in humans? God's attributes are a matter for praise; but how can we praise God for being jealous?"[2]

Dr. Packer then makes two helpful observations.

First we have to recognize the limitations of human language about God. The Bible uses language and imagery drawn from our personal lives because we can more easily understand God on such terms. But we have to always remember, "when language of human personal life is used of God none of the limitations of human creaturehood are thereby being implied."[3] So in contrast to much human jealousy, God's jealousy is not "a compound of frustration, envy, and spite."[4]

Second, Dr. Packer reminds us that there are two kinds of human jealousy, one to be avoided, and the other to be fully exercised. The first kind is the jealousy born out of resentment; resentment that others have what I want. Such jealousy is sin, a cousin of coveting. The second kind of jealousy is born out of zeal to protect a love relationship, and to avenge (!) it when it is broken.[5] Married persons "who felt no jealousy at the intrusion

---

1 A. Stumpff, *Theological Dictionary of the New Testament Vol.II* (Grand Rapids: Eerdmans, 1964), 884.
2 J. I. Packer, *Knowing God* (Downers Grove: Inter-Varsity Press, 1973), 152.
3 Ibid.
4 Ibid.
5 Ibid, 154.

of a lover or an adulterer into their home would surely be lacking in moral perfection, for the exclusiveness of marriage is the essence of marriage."[6] God's jealousy is of the second kind: it is "a praiseworthy zeal to preserve something supremely precious."[7]

In the first commandment, "You shall have no other gods before Me," Yahweh is jealous to keep us from ruining our lives by worshiping anyone or anything other than the One for whom we were created and redeemed. In the second commandment, "You shall not make for yourself an idol, or any likeness..." Yahweh is jealous *to keep us from ruining our lives worshiping the Living God in ways that actually get in the way.*

As we did with the first commandment let us dig deeper by asking four questions of this second commandment:

1. What is the nature of the images, the likenesses, Yahweh prohibits?

2. What is it about Yahweh's being that makes worshiping with images so inappropriate?

3. How does the use of images and likenesses affect our relationship with Yahweh?

4. How then are we to relate to Yahweh? Does God give us any help in light of our human need for some sort of visualization?

---

6 R.V.G. Tasker, *The General Epistle of James, An Introduction and Commentary* (Grand Rapids: Eerdmans, 1957), 106.
7 Packer, op.cit.

1. First question: *What is the nature of the images Yahweh prohibits? What exactly is God commanding us* **not** *to do?*

The word translated "images" (or "idol") is related to the Hebrew verb meaning "to carve." "Image" refers to figures or statues carved out of wood. God is referring first of all to wooden idols, which—as we see in the prophets, especially Isaiah—were a major problem. But the rest of Scripture expands the idea of "image" to include idols made of molten iron, which were also a major problem. When we keep reading the Bible, we discover that the Biblical authors expand the word to include images of God drawn or painted on canvas. Eventually the word includes images, likenesses of God, drawn on our minds by our imaginations.

So the second commandment warns us against any and all human-made images of God: be they statues, paintings, or mental pictures.

2. Which raises the second question: *What is it about God's being that makes worshiping with images so inappropriate?*

More specifically, what about Yahweh's mode of being makes image making inappropriate?

Moses, to whom the Ten Commandments were first spoken, gives us part of the answer in the book of Deuteronomy (*deutero* = second, *nomos* = law; Deuteronomy = second telling of the Law). Moses is reminding the Israelites about the events surrounding the giving of the Law:

Remember the day you stood before Yahweh at Horeb...you came near and stood at the foot of the mountain, and the mountain burned with fire to the very heart of the heavens: darkness, cloud and thick gloom. Then Yahweh spoke to you from the midst of the fire; you heard the sound of words, but you saw no form—only a voice.

Deuteronomy 4:10–12

The key line is the last: "You heard the sound of words, but *you saw no form—only a voice.*" Then Moses says:

So watch yourselves carefully, since you did not see any form... lest you act corruptly and make a graven image for yourselves, in the form of any figure, the likeness of male or female, the likeness of any animal that is on the earth, the likeness of any winged bird that flies in the sky, the likeness of anything that creeps on the ground, the likeness of any fish that is in the water below the earth. And beware, lest you lift up your eyes to heaven, and see the sun and the moon and the stars, all the host of heaven, and be drawn away and worship them and serve them, those which Yahweh your God has allotted to all the peoples under the whole heaven.

Deuteronomy 4:15–19

Because Israel saw no form when Yahweh descended on the mountain (Yahweh had no form to be seen), but only heard Yahweh's voice (Yahweh's Word), any image of God—any visible likeness of God from creation or made by human beings—ignores the mode of God's being and self-revelation.

Old Testament scholar, Brevard Childs, then summarizes

Moses' point: "Images are prohibited because they are an incorrect response to God's manner of making Himself known, which was by means of His Word."[8]

The whole matter goes even deeper. Notice in the second commandment the references to creation: heaven above, earth below, water beneath the earth, and everything that exists in those spheres. We are to make no images, or likenesses, of anything in heaven above, on earth below, or in the waters beneath. Why? Because although everything is created by Yahweh the Lawgiver, none of it is Yahweh the Lawgiver. Creation is not God. The work of God, yes. But not God. Creation is not even, as some religious systems hold, an extension of God. God holds it all together, moment-by-moment. But none of it is an extension of God. Therefore, nothing in creation can serve as an image of God; nothing in creation can represent God; nothing in creation can stand in God's place and reveal God as God really is.

Yes, creation bears the stamp of God's handiwork; we see God's "fingerprints" everywhere! Creation declares the power and wisdom and glories of God. Creation reflects God's glory. But none of it is God. None of it is an extension of God's being.

Therefore, again, nothing in creation can possibly be the image and likeness of God: nothing in the heaven—no star, no moon, no sun—(contrary to what the Persians thought); nothing in the sea—no fish, no sea monster—(contrary to what the Babylonians thought); nothing on earth—no animal, no bird (contrary to what the Egyptians and Greeks thought).

But, what about us? Does not Genesis, Chapter One, call us

---

8 Brevard S. Childs, *The Book of Exodus: A Critical, Theological Commentary* (Philadelphia: Westminster Press, 1974), 407.

humans, male and female, the image of God?" No. Read the text carefully. Then God said, "Let us make humanity in Our image, according to Our likeness" (Genesis 1:26). "In." "According to." We are not God's image—God's likeness. We are created in God's image, *according to* God's likeness. We are image-bearers. We reflect the glory of God, better than anything else in creation. But we are *not* the glory of God. We manifest something of the nature and character of God, better than anything else in creation. But we are *not* the nature and character of God. *Nothing in creation is God; and, therefore, nothing in creation can serve as the image of God.*

This is one of the implications of calling God "Holy." Holy means pure. But Holy also, and primarily, means "other than." "God is Holy," means God is *other than* the created order.

This radical distinction between the Creator and the creation is played out in an experience the prophet Elijah had. After running away in fear from Jezebel, Elijah hid himself in a cave. God called him to stand on the mountain. Then we read in 1 Kings 19:11–12:

> ...And behold [look!], Yahweh was passing by! And a great and strong wind was rending the mountains and breaking in pieces the rocks before Yahweh; but Yahweh was not in the wind. And after the wind an earthquake, but Yahweh was not in the earthquake. And after the earthquake a fire, but Yahweh was not in the fire; and after the fire a sound of gentle blowing.

The wind, earthquake and fire signaled that Yahweh was present. But Yahweh was not in them. Israel's contemporaries thought otherwise. So do many religious and philosophical systems of our day.

Old Testament scholar, Gerhard von Rad pulls together the point I am wanting to make. "We shall be on the right track if, with Israel's religious environment in mind, we understand the (second) commandment as the expression of an utterly different view of the world. ...In the greater and the lesser religions of the ancient East, the gods were personified powers of heaven or earth or the abyss. But this was not the way in which Yahweh was related to the world. However powerful his sway in it was, theologically he still transcended it. Nature was not a mode of Yahweh's being; he stood over against it as its Creator."[9] Since creation is other than God and since it is not an extension of God, we can find in creation no image or likeness of God. All images of God, drawn from creation, made by human beings—by the imagining creature—fall short of God's glory.

3. Which brings us to the third question: *How does the use of images affect our relationship with Yahweh?*

The answer is straightforward. Images put God in a box. We are, therefore, no longer relating to the true God. We are relating to *less than* the true God, and in extreme cases, relating to *other than* the true God.

Images put God in a box in at least four ways, each messing up our relationship with God.

(A) First, every image taken from creation *limits God*. For the simple reason that no one image can possibly paint the whole picture. At best, it can only paint one little part of the picture. If

---

9 Gerhard von Rad, *Old Testament Theology, Vol. 1* (Edinburgh: Oliver and Boyd, 1962), 218.

I use that one image in my worship of God, my vision of God is severely distorted. For that one image blocks me off from other aspects of God's nature and character. Then instead of helping me see God, the image actually blinds me to God. "The heart of the objection to pictures and images is that they inevitably conceal most, if not all, of the truth about the personal nature and character of the divine Being whom they represent."[10]

Let me illustrate. Take the image of a bull. A bull could stand for the strength and durability of God. But, if we worshiped God using only the image of the bull, we would miss out on God as lamb, pointing to God's gentleness, or miss out on God as fire, pointing to God's purity and cleansing presence. Using the image of the bull alone blinds us to other dimensions of God's nature and character.

The same is true of the use of mental images of God. Every human-made mental conception of God is inadequate. It may be true, but by itself it is inadequate. If I focus on God using only that mental image, I slowly, but surely, have a God who is too small.

This fact about images tells us we need to be careful even when working with Biblical images of God. No one image tells us everything. If we stay with just one image, we box God in. "God is on the throne": it is the dominant image of the book of Revelation. Thank God, God is on the throne. There is never a time when God is not on the throne. But if I only hang on to that image, as true as it is, I will miss out on the equally true and powerful image of God on His knees, sacrificing Himself in service to us.

10 Packer, op.cit., 40.

When one image, especially one from creation, takes over our vision, our vision is limited.

(B) Secondly, every image taken from creation leads us astray. For we can easily begin to think that other things in the image are also true about God. Take the example of the bull again. Aaron, Moses' brother, built the golden bull calf, and then pointing at it said, "This is your god, O Israel, who brought you up from the land of Egypt" (Exodus 32:4). Aaron no doubt chooses the bull to honor Yahweh as the God of power. But the bull was also a symbol of virility, of sexual prowess. If Israel kept that statue long enough, Israel would begin to think of God in those other terms as well. And sooner or later, Israel would adopt forms of worship involving sexual intercourse.

Which is what happened to the Greeks. They saw the gods in terms of men and women. At first, those images simply taught them that the gods were, like men and women, personal and rational beings. But soon the gods took on all of the other aspects of human nature, especially sexual desire. Worship then took on sexual overtones until the Greeks developed the form of worship involving sexual intercourse with temple prostitutes. Their images had led them astray.

Take another example, "The Force" of Star Wars. "The Force" is the god element in the movies. The concept of the Force, as George Lucas develops it, does teach us many true things about the Living God. But the concept also leads us astray, for "The Force" is both good and evil. "The Force" has both a good and evil side. Which is not true of the Living God. There is *no evil* in God. Evil is outside of God, other than God, anti-God. Which is why the true God gives us hope. The true God is bigger than evil. Good does win in the end. The Star Wars "god" offers no hope. For even within "The Force" itself there is no certainty of the victory of good. Every human-made image ultimately leads us astray.

(C) Thirdly, images box God in because images *localize* God. That is, I come to think that I meet God in the box, at the statue, in the picture, in the mental image. This was the primary function of idols in Israel's time. People in the ancient East were fully aware that their images of the deity were inadequate. But, as inadequate as they were, people still felt that the image was the place where the deity "broke through" to them. The image became the point of contact with God. Thus different peoples had their sacred rocks, their sacred mountains, and their sacred relics.

You can see how dangerous this is. For I can then come to think that I meet God *only* in such and such a place, *only* while holding such and such a relic in my hands, *only* while focusing on such and such painting or *only* while thinking such and such a mental image of God. The woman who Jesus met at the well seems to have had just such a view of God. She said to Jesus: "Our fathers [the Samaritans] worshiped on this mountain; and you people [the Jews] say that in Jerusalem is the place where we ought to worship." Jesus said to her, "Woman, believe Me, an hour is coming when neither on this mountain, nor in Jerusalem, shall you worship the Father. "...But an hour is coming, and now is, when the true worshipers will worship the Father in spirit and truth; for such people the Father seeks to be His worshipers. God is Spirit, and those who worship Him must worship in spirit and truth" (John 4:20–24).

Jesus freed her, and us, from a false concept of God. Jesus freed her from her image which localized God.

(D) Fourthly, images box God in because they finally *become a substitute for God.* If I live long enough with the idea that I meet God in a particular statue or picture, the statue or picture will become God to me.

It actually happened in Israel's experience. At one point during the wandering in the desert, in response to the people's unrepentant sin, God sent serpents among them. The people begged Moses to beg God to remove the serpents. God then told Moses to make a bronze serpent and set it up on a pole. "It shall come about," said God, "that everyone who is bitten, when he looks at [the bronze serpent on the pole], he shall live" (Numbers 21:6–9). In no way did God intend the serpent to substitute for God. Yet years later some of the Israelites worshiped the serpent, burning incense before it (2 Kings 18:4).

The story illustrates all four dangers of human-made images. They limit our vision of God, they lead us astray, we begin to think of them as the contact point with the Divine God and they slowly become a substitute for the Divine God. What mercy and grace is behind the speaking of the second commandment: "You shall not make for yourself any image, or any likeness."

Human-made images affect *our* relationship with God. But the second commandment also tells us that our images affect *other* peoples' relationships with God. How?

> "...I, Yahweh your God, am a jealous God, visiting the iniquity of the fathers on the children, on the third and fourth generations of those who hate me, but showing loving kindness to thousands of generations to those who love Me and keep My commandments."
>
> Exodus 20:5–6

The point? There are many. One of them being that our false concepts—our images and likenesses of God—are passed on to our children. Our children pick them up without us saying a word. For we automatically relate to other people out of our vision of God.

So, for example, if a father's image of God is of a God who is never really satisfied with our service, the father is never free to rest and enjoy God and God's goodness. That father's daughter will adopt, implicitly, the same vision. She, too, never allows herself to rest—to enter into the rest God offers God's people by grace.

Another example is a mother's image of God. She tells her daughter she has to have it all together before God will love her. She then treats her son the same way, telling him, "I love you" only when he is good, or when he succeeds. The son then goes into life with the same vision. And so you hear his response to the invitation to come to the Lord's Table by saying, "I am not good enough yet." His inherited image of God keeps him from hearing that the Lord's Table is precisely for those who do not have their life together.

"You shall not make for yourself any image or any likeness." It is spoken for our sake and for our children's sake.

We need to make it very clear that the second commandment does not prohibit the use of art in worship. It does not call us to worship God in a room stripped bare of symbols. How do I know this? Because the God of the second commandment ordered Israel to build the Tabernacle. Read Exodus 25–40 sometime, and you will see how God painstakingly describes all of the ways that place of worship is to be adorned. It was to be filled with color, texture and symbols. God speaks of the Holy Spirit coming upon and enabling certain people to do the work of carving and designing and embroidering (Exodus 35:31ff.). The God of the second commandment also ordered that we celebrate the Lord's Supper, using the symbols of bread and wine, both taken from creation, eloquently proclaiming mercy and grace.

But note carefully that the art forms in the Tabernacle and the symbols in the Lord's Supper intentionally point away from themselves—beyond themselves—toward the Living God. The cherubim, the angelic beings, who stand over the Ark of the Covenant in the Holy of Holies, have wings that cover their eyes, telling us that we cannot see the Living God in all of God's glory. Yet! Indeed, as one moves through the Tabernacle, room by room, further and further toward the Holy of Holies, the symbolism decreases, until at the place where the high priest meets God there is nothing.[11] It is open space, proclaiming very graphically that nothing in all of creation can finally stand in God's place as God.

4. We come to the fourth question: *How then are we to relate to the Invisible God?*

If our human-made images distort and lead astray, what are we to do? Given our apparently universal need for some sort of visualization of the Divine, what are we to do?

I have some very exciting news for you. The Living God knows us. God knows our need for some visual aid. Since God wants us to know God as God really is, God gives us an image

---

11 I heard someone put it that way, but do not remember who.

of God's Self. *We* cannot make an image of God. But *God* can. And God does.

Listen to the following affirmation from the New Testament:

For God, who said, "Light shall shine out of darkness," is the One who has shone in our hearts to give us the light of the knowledge of the glory of God in the face of Christ.

2 Corinthians 4:6

And He is the image of the invisible God....

Colossians 1:15

And He is the radiance of God's glory and the exact representation of God's nature....

Hebrews 1:3

Did you hear that? *We* cannot make an image or likeness of God. But *God* can. God can construct an icon (that is the word used in 2 Corinthians and Colossians) that is God's exact likeness. *The icon of God is Jesus Christ!* Jesus is not only like us, in the image of God. He *is* the image of God. The Invisible, Hidden, Un-imaginable God, has made *the perfect image*, the perfect likeness, and it turns out to be Jesus of Nazareth.

If you will, *God puts God in a box.* A box of God's own choosing and making. But this box (if we can rightly speak this way) avoids the four dangers of human-made images.

(A) For, first of all, Jesus is the one image who *does not limit God's glory.* What we see in Jesus does not blind us to God's true character. As John says, "The Word became flesh, and dwelt among us, and we beheld His glory, glory as of the only begotten from the Father, full of grace and truth" (John 1:14). "No one has seen God at any time; the only begotten God [Jesus], who is in the bosom of the Father, He has explained God" (John 1:18).

(B) Secondly, Jesus Christ is the one image of God that *does not lead us astray*. What we see in Jesus is all true of the Invisible God. Jesus says, "They who behold Me behold the One who sent Me" (John 12:45).

(C) Thirdly, Jesus Christ is the one image of God *where we do meet* God. Paul says, "God was in Christ reconciling the world to Himself" (2 Corinthians 5:19). Jesus says, "The one who has seen Me has seen the Father" (John 14:9). Jesus *is the point of contact* with the Invisible God.

(D) And fourthly, Jesus Christ is *the one image of God that really* is God. Paul says, "In Him [Christ] all the fullness of Deity dwells in bodily form" (Colossians 2:9). Jesus says, "I and the Father are one" (John 10:30).

We are not left to our imaginations! God gives us an image of God's Self that is God. Jesus Christ, fully human, is fully God. He is one icon/image/likeness of God we can worship and serve and not commit idolatry (see 1 John 5:20–21).

Therefore, I submit to you that we can restate the second commandment positively. In place of the negative, "You shall not make for yourself any image," we can put the positive, *"Behold My Son!"*[12] Behold Jesus Christ. In Him you do see Me. Love Him and you will not be putting Me in a box."

---

12 Note that in the Gospels every time the Father speaks He speaks about His Son! At His baptism, "This is My beloved Son, in whom I am well pleased" (Matthew 3:17); at His transfiguration, "This is My beloved Son, with whom I am well pleased; listen to Him!" (Matthew 17:5). See also how the author of Hebrews reads a number of Old Testament texts (Hebrews 1:5-13).

Here, too, we need to be careful. For it is all too easy to also put God's image in a box. Thank God, Jesus won't stay in any of the boxes long. As C. S. Lewis has one of the children say in the "The Lion, The Witch, and the Wardrobe" (of the *Chronicles of Narnia*), "He's not a tame lion, you know." If we keep the focus on Jesus, we will be moving in the right direction. And in the process He will slowly, but surely, overcome all of our inadequate imaginings.

Let me conclude this chapter by suggesting three practical implications of obeying the second commandment.

(1) First, obeying the commandment protects and enhances the unity of the Church. The Living God is so much bigger than any one denomination's images. The Living God is bigger than all the images of all the denominations combined. No one has a corner on God. No one can point to that box and say, "This is God." No one can point to this box and say, "This is Jesus." When we recognize the inadequacy of our vision of God, we find the humility to listen to other believers. And then together we find the humility to subject *all* of our visions to the Word of God.

(2) Second, obeying the second commandment will *expand* our vision of God, and, therefore, of life. Our worlds are as big as our vision of God. The God who comes to us as Jesus Christ is the God who knows when a sparrow falls to the ground and the God who sets up and takes down empires and civilizations. The God who comes to us as Jesus Christ is the God who knows the number of hairs on our head, and He is the God who counts all of the stars of the universe. The more our little images of God are smashed under the weight of God's image, Jesus Christ, the bigger God becomes. A God big enough to hold the world together. A God big enough to hold *our lives* together.

(3) Third, obeying the second commandment will result in changed lives. For we become like what we worship. We become like what we idolize. That simply is the way it is. Here is the promise: "But we all, with unveiled face beholding as in a mirror the glory of the Lord, are being transformed into the same image from glory to glory..." (2 Corinthians 3:18). The more we focus on God's image of God, on Jesus, the more we become like Him, which means, the more we become who we were created to be. For Jesus is at once the perfect revelation of God and the perfect revelation of who we, through Him, were created and redeemed to be.[13]

The words of an old hymn give verbal expression to what my heart wants to say to the God of the second commandment:

Be Thou my vision, O Lord of my heart;
Naught be all else to me, save that Thou art.[14]

O Living God, do not be anything else to me but who You *really* are. Oh Jealous God, do not let me box you in.

---

13 In 1928, a number of Christian leaders (including William Temple, Robert Speer, John R. Mott and John MacKay) spent fifteen days on the Mount of Olives for what was called The International Missionary conference. The opening line of their summary report was, "Our message is Jesus Christ. He is the revelation of what God is and what man, through Jesus, may become."
14 "Be Thou My Vision," Traditional Irish hymn, circa 8th century; translated by Mary E. Byrne, 1905; verses added by Elenor Hull, 1912; Hope Publishing, 1974.

EXODUS 20:7

"You shall not take the name of the Lord your God in vain, for the Lord will not leave the person unpunished who takes His name in vain."

DON'T LET IT BE IN VAIN

What a different world this would be if more of us were living this third commandment.

I had thought about subtitling this chapter, "Something Worse Than Profanity." For as I hope to demonstrate, using God's name to express anger or frustration or surprise is *the least offensive* way the third commandment is broken. It turns out that people who *know* the God who has a name break the commandment more than people who do *not know* the God who has a name but use the name in profanity.

Why did the Living God speak the third commandment? Because God does not want to see us waste a precious gift. Precious is an understatement. In the third commandment, the Living God is saying, "I have given you one of the greatest gifts you can ever receive. Do not take it in vain."

The Hebrew word translated "vain" literally means "nothing" or "emptiness." "O give us help against the adversary, for deliverance by human beings is in vain" [the word is emptiness] (Psalm 60:11).

Unless the Lord builds the house,

They labor in vain who build it;

Unless the Lord guards the city,

The watchman keeps awake in vain [for nothing].

Psalm 127:1

In the third commandment, the Living God is saying to Moses, to old Israel, to new Israel (the Church), to you and to me, "I have given you something supremely precious...something for which I am very jealous. I have given you something that changes your life. Do not let it be for nothing. Do not empty it of its richness and power. Do not take my gift in vain."

And what is the gift? It is God's name. The Living and Holy God has a name. A personal name. A first name, if you will. And God has told us what it is. And God has invited us to take it. The word "take" in this commandment means to "carry," to "raise," to "take up." The Living and Holy God has a name, has told us what it is, and has invited us to take it up and use it.

Review the context.

Only a few months before God spoke the Ten Commandments from Mt. Sinai, God encountered Moses at the foot of the mountain in a burning bush. The encounter is described in Exodus 3. From within the bush, aflame with fire but not being consumed, the Living God spoke surprising words. God said, "Moses...I am the God of your father, the God of Abraham, the God of Isaac, and the God of Jacob.... I have surely seen the affliction of My people who are in Egypt, and have given heed to their cry because of their taskmasters, for I am aware of their sufferings. So I have come down to deliver them..." (Exodus 3:4, 6–8).

They are revolutionary words in any generation. It meant

DON'T LET IT BE IN VAIN

that Israel's four hundred years of slavery and oppression had not gone unnoticed. Her prayers had been heard. She had not been alone in her suffering. The God of her ancestors, the God of Abraham and Sarah, the God of Isaac and Rebecca, the God of Jacob and Rachael and Leah, is the God who *sees* everything that happens in our worlds, who *hears* the cries of agony and despair, who *feels* the world's pain, and who *comes down* to intervene on behalf of His people.

So surprising—so wonderfully surprising—is this revelation that Moses asks God, "Who are You?" But like a good Middle Easterner, he does not ask it directly. He asks the question in a roundabout way. Moses says: "Behold, I am going to the sons of Israel, and I shall say to them, 'The God of your fathers has sent me to you.' Now they may say to me, 'What is His name?' What shall I say to them?" (Exodus 3:13).

God responds: "I AM WHO I AM. ...Thus you shall say to the sons of Israel, 'I AM has sent me to you'" (Exodus 3:14). God continues: "Thus you shall say to the sons of Israel, 'Yahweh, [this is the name buried beneath the words "The LORD"], the God of your fathers, the God of Abraham, the God of Isaac and the God of Jacob, has sent me to you.' This is My name forever, the name by which I am to be remembered from generation to generation" (Exodus 3:15).

According to Australian Old Testament scholar, Francis I. Andersen, the two greatest moments in history are (1) when the Living God revealed His name, Yahweh; and (2) when the Living God came down to us in Person bearing the name Yeshua, Jesus, which means "Yahweh Is Salvation," Yahweh to the Rescue."[1]

---

1 In a lecture I heard him give.

When God revealed God's Self to Moses' ancestors in the past, God became known by a name, or a title, which in some way conveyed that revelation. The most important name up to this point in Israel's history was *El-Shaddai*. *El-Shaddai* is made up of two words, "*El*," the common Semitic term for the Divine, and "*Shaddai*," which means "Mighty One." Up to this point in history Israel had experienced the Living One as "Almighty God."

But at the burning bush, God was revealing something more. The God of Abraham, Isaac, and Jacob, sees and hears and feels people's suffering, and chooses to get involved with and intervene for His people. *This is new revelation!* Therefore, Moses and the Israelites expect a new name or title. The titles by which God was called up to this point in history could not convey the new revelation. Thus the question, "What is Your name?"

"My name is Yahweh." I want you to call Me Yahweh.

In the Ancient Near East, names carried greater significance than they do today. You did not know a person unless you knew his or her name. A name in some way expressed the person's essential character or told you something about the person's history (past, present, or future).

So, for example, Nabal in Hebrew means, "fool." When you read the story of Nabal's life, you see how magnificently he lived up to his name (1 Samuel 25:25)! Eve, the name of the first woman, means, "mother of all living" (Genesis 3:20). Isaac means, "laughter," reminding us that his parents laughed when God told them they would conceive a child even though they were both over ninety years old (Genesis 17:17; 18:12).

The significance of names is illustrated more forcefully when names were changed. Abram becomes Abraham, meaning "father of many nations" (Genesis 17:5). Jacob becomes Israel, which means, "he wrestled with *El*, with God" (Genesis 32:28). Simon, a name related to the word for shifting sand, became Peter, which means, "rock" (John 1:42). A name tells us something about the character or history of the person so named.

Names in the Ancient Near East also carried greater significance than they do today because it was thought that if you knew the name of a being (whether that being was a human, an angel, or demon, or a god) you could, supposedly, exert power over it.[2] One was, therefore, very careful about giving her name to another person. She was, in effect, giving the other person a hold on her life.

Furthermore, in some cultures to give one's name to another meant that you were establishing a relationship in which all that your name implied is at the disposal of the other.

Frederick Buechner, a Presbyterian pastor/author, pulls all of these ideas about "name" together when he speaks of his own name.

> B-u-e-c-h-n-e-r. It is my name. It is pronounced Beckner. If somebody mispronounces it in some foolish way, I have the feeling that what is foolish is me. If somebody forgets it, I feel that it is I who am forgotten. There is something about it that embarrasses me in just the same way that there is something about me that embarrasses me. I cannot imagine myself with any other name—Held, say, or Merrill, or Hlavacek. If my name were different, I would be different. When I tell somebody my name, I have given him a hold over me that he did not have before. If he calls it out, I stop, look, and listen whether I want

---

2 H. Bietenhard, "Onama", *TDNT*, Vol. V, 253.

to or not. In the Book of Exodus, God tells Moses his name is Yahweh, and God hasn't had a peaceful moment since.[3]

And that is perfectly fine with God. God wants to be known. God lets us know and use God's name. Yahweh, Y-a-h-w-e-h. "This is My name forever, the name by which I am to be remembered from generation to generation" (Exodus 3:15).

"You shall not take the name of Yahweh your God in vain."

"Yahweh." Biblical scholars are not one hundred percent sure that that is the correct pronunciation. This uncertainty is due to the fact that Biblical Hebrew does not have written vowels; only the consonants are written down. The consonants of God's name are Y-H-W-H. Moses knew which vowels were to be vocalized between those consonants. And for a few generations after Moses, everyone who knew God knew the correct pronunciation. Somewhere along the line, however, strict Jews stopped uttering the sacred name. They were afraid lest they transgress the third commandment. So whenever they were reading Scripture out loud and came across Yahweh, they substituted another word. Most often they substituted the word "*Adonai*" meaning "my Lord." But soon the fear of breaking the third commandment led to further substitutions (circumlocutions) such as "heaven," or "the place," or even simply "the name," *ha-shēm.* Some superstrict Jews even avoided using *ha-shēm,* and just spoke the letters "*h*," or "*hē.*" In the process, the original vocalization of the four consonants Y-H-W-H was lost.

In recent centuries, the Church has thought that "Jehovah" was the proper vocalization. We find that form in a number of

---

3 Frederick Buechner, *Wishful Thinking* (New York: Harper & Row, 1973), 12.

our hymns, "Guide Me, O Thou Great Jehovah," for example. How did the Church come up with that vocalization? A group of rabbis took the vowels from the substitute word "*Adonai*" and inserted them between the consonants Y-H-W-H. (Y and W can be rendered J and V). But according to Paul Jewett what we need to realize is that the rabbis did this "deliberately to thwart the pronunciation of the ineffable name of God"![4]

Thus, scholars today realize "Jehovah" is not correct. The better vocalization is "Yahweh."

Most English versions of the Bible continue the Jewish reluctance to utter God's name by rendering it with the term LORD, all letters capitalized. LORD is the English translation of the Greek word Kurios which translates the Hebrew word *Adonai*, "my Lord." I understand and appreciate the motive for rendering the sacred name in this way. But God wants to be called by name! "God" is not God's name. It is a generic term, telling us what God is. "The Lord" is not God's name. It is a title. So are other terms like Rock, Shepherd, Light, Alpha and Omega. My title is "The Reverend Mr. Johnson." When people call me that I feel important. My name is "Darrell." When people call me that I feel like a person. I do not call my wife, Sharon, "the wife." I call her "Sharon." The Living God wants and likes to be called by name. "My name is Yahweh."

The fact is that the Church, and the Synagogue, regularly use the sacred name. A central word of our worship vocabulary is "Hallelujah." It is made up of two Hebrew words; "*hallelu*" meaning "you praise," and "*yah*," the short form of Yahweh.

---

4 From an unpublished lecture, Fuller Theological Seminary, 'Systematic Theology,' Winter 1970.

Hallelujah equals praise Yahweh!

"You shall not take the name of Yahweh your God in vain."

Before exploring what taking the name in vain entails, let us ask, *what does the name mean?*

Again, Biblical scholars are not one hundred percent certain. The word "Yahweh" is a verb. It is derived from the verb "*hayah,*" which means "to be." But, "to be" in what sense? The verb "Yahweh" can mean either "He is," or "He causes to be" (either a simple-stem verb or a causative-stem verb). On purely grammatical grounds it can go either way.[5]

I think, however, that God's extended answer to the question Moses raised, "What is Your name?" helps us decide. "God said to Moses 'I AM WHO I AM'; and He said, 'Thus you shall say to the sons of Israel, "I AM has sent me to you"'" (Exodus 3:14). The phrases "I AM WHO I AM" and "I AM" interpret the name Yahweh. And those phases cannot be rendered, "I cause to be what I cause to be."

The Greek version of the Old Testament, the Septuagint, saw this and so rendered "I AM WHO I AM" as "I Am the One Who is." The verb "Yahweh" simply means, "He is." From within the burning bush the Holy One claims to be "The One Who really is."

However, this is not to be understood in a Western way, through the Greek understanding of reality. It must be understood in an Eastern way, through the Hebrew understanding of reality. When God says, 'I AM WHO I AM," the Old Testament and New Testament authors did not think in abstract philosophical categories. Not "I am the elusive One." Not even "I am pure being." The Hebrew tradition thinks in relational terms. "He is"

---

5 Ibid.

in the Hebrew mind means, "He is the One Who is really there, with us and for us." The emphasis in the name Yahweh is not on pure existence, but on being present.[6] "*I Am the One Who is really there, with you and for you.*"

The Hebrew language does not have tenses like the English past, present and future. So the Hebrew phrase which interprets the verb "Yahweh" can be rendered in all three tenses: "I am Who I am; I was Who I was; I will be Who I will be." All of that is meant by God's name. "I am Yahweh, the One Who is; the One Who is there with you and for you; the One Who was there with you and for you; the One Who will be there with you and for you."

That is why Yahweh is the God Who *sees* and *hears* and *feels* and finally *comes down.*

Now, the fact of the matter is, the name will not be fully understood until Moses walks with God for a while. The meaning of the name is not clear until God acts in the history of Israel. Indeed, the meaning of the name will not be finally understood until Yahweh comes to us in Person, as Jesus of Nazareth. Jesus, Yeshua, is God's name taken to the full extent of its meaning: for Jesus is Yahweh with us and for us in our flesh and blood.

"My name is Yahweh." The gift of the name is an invitation to relationship. It means God is giving us God's own self. God is giving us full access to all that the name implies.

"You shall not take the name of Yahweh your God in vain."

The question is then, *how do we take God's name in vain?* How do we empty it, making it of no value? The question is intensified by what God says after commanding us not to take the name in vain: "...for Yahweh will not leave unpunished the one who takes

---

6 I owe this insight to Martin Noth.

His name in vain." Since we cannot separate God's name and God's person, to take God's name in vain is to take God in vain! To waste the gift of the name is to waste the gift of God's self.

There are many ways we break the third commandment. I am going to explore only three. Along with each of them, I will identify its opposite, i.e., the way we keep the third commandment. Three negative uses of the name and then three positive uses of the name.

(1) First, I take up God's name in vain when I treat God's name as a magic formula. Many of Israel's contemporaries believed that simply by uttering the consonants and vowels of the Deity's name, one could get the Deity's attention and exercise control over it. Simply uttering the name conjured up the god's power and blessing.

For Israel's contemporaries there was in actual fact no way to speak a god's name in vain. If one called upon his or her god using the right name, "Things started to happen!"[7] The third commandment challenges the prevailing view: simply knowing and uttering God's name was no guarantee of God's response. It is possible to utter the sacred name and it means nothing at all. The third commandment teaches that "Yahweh, even when addressed as Yahweh, cannot be controlled or manipulated. God's name is spoken in vain when we think we can get God to do our bidding just because we spoke it. Yahweh refuses to be conjured up by the utterance of the name."[8]

Even though we modern believers understand this, we still

---

7 JoyDavidman, *Smoke on the Mountain: An Interpretation of the Ten Commandments* (Philadelphia: Westminster Press, 1954),42.
8 Biethenhard, op.cit.

try to use God's name in a magical way. The chief way we still treat the name as a magic formula is by taking oaths in God's name. We add to our promise "By God I will do it," or; "So help me God, that's the truth," hoping thereby to guarantee the oath, or to magically transform a false promise into the truth.

Such use of God's name empties the name. It makes it nothing. Which is why Jesus commands us in His Sermon on the Mount not to bring God into it at all! "Let your 'yes' be 'yes,' and your 'no' be 'no'" (Matthew 5:33–37). Adding the word "God" does not do anything for the oath, and only cheapens God in the process.

That is the negative, now the positive.

Although God's name is not a magical word it does, nevertheless, carry weighty authority. God's name does make things happen! The prophets prefaced their messages with "Thus says the Lord," "Thus says Yahweh," because of the conviction that the name carries clout in the universe. Somehow, even creation itself comes to attention at the name of Yahweh—even if only to disobey the word in the next moment. We sing rightly, "The mountains bow down and the seas will roar at the sound of Your name."[9] And demons flee and the dead rise up at the sound of the name.

We see the authority of the name lived out in the experience of the early Church. For example, one day, Peter and John went to the temple to pray. As they climbed the steps, a lame man began begging them for alms. Peter looked at him and said, "I do not possess silver and gold, but what I do have I give to you:

9 Darlene Zschech, "Shout to the Lord." *People Just Like Us*. Hillsong Music Australia, 1994.

In the name of Jesus Christ the Nazarene—walk!" (Acts 3:1–9). And the man stood up and walked! Another example is when Paul was in the city of Philippi. A girl caught up in the occult, and exploited as a fortune teller by some wealthy men, kept following Paul, raising a ruckus. After it became clear to Paul that the girl was overtaken by an evil spirit, Paul turned to her and said to the Spirit, "I command you in the name of Jesus Christ to come out of her!" And the girl was free (Acts 16:16–18).

The name "Yahweh," the name "Yeshua," Jesus, carries clout in the spiritual realm. It carries clout in the whole universe. As Paul says in Philippians 2:10–11, one day "...at the name of Jesus every knee shall bow of those who are in heaven, on the earth, and under the earth, and that every tongue should confess that Jesus Christ is Lord, to the glory of God the Father." In His name we disciples can come against the evil and chaos around us. Principalities and powers, rulers and authorities, must submit to the name. So Martin Luther can sing:

> And though this world, with devils filled,
> Should threaten to undo us,
> We will not fear, for God hath willed
> His truth to triumph through us.
> The prince of darkness grim,
> We tremble not for him;
> His rage we can endure,
> For lo! His doom is sure:
> One little word shall fell him.[10]

That "one little word" is a name: "Lord Sabaoth His name."

---

10 His hymn, "A Mighty Fortress is Our God".

Jesus shall fell the prince of darkness.

We take the name in vain when we treat it as a magic formula. We take up the name in honor—in fullness—when we trust its inherent authority.

(2) Secondly, I take the name of God in vain when I live in a way that does not square with the name. Time after time, the prophets charged Israel of old with blaspheming God's name by the way they were living (Isaiah 52:5). How often the Church has brought shame on the name by the way we live! The world dismisses the name either as the source of the trouble or as irrelevant. I cannot even count the times people have brought up the Crusades, or the Church's silence in Nazi Germany, or the building of lavish cathedrals in slum areas, or by the fact that North American believers spend more money feeding our pets than we do alleviating world hunger. We can empty the name, make it nothing in the world, by the way we, who know the name, live. Friedrich Neitzsche, the German existentialist philosopher, once said, "Show me that you are redeemed and then I will believe in your redeemer." Mahatma Gandhi said to E. Stanley Jones, "I like what I see in your Christ; it is you Christians that cause me trouble."[11]

That is the negative, now the positive.

We take up the name of God in honor, in fullness, when we do live a life consistent with Yahweh's character. "You shall be holy for I, Yahweh your God, am Holy" (Leviticus 19:2). As we noted in the last chapter, we become like our gods. We become like that which we truly worship.

So Jesus teaches us to pray: "Our Father who art in heaven,

---

11 E. Stanley Jones, *Gandhi: Portrait of a Friend* (New York, Cincinnati [etc.]: The Abingdon Press, 1982, 2019).

hallowed be Your name, ...on earth as it is in heaven." Literally, "hallow Your name." It is a request that God do something about His name. O Living God, please make Your name real on earth as it is in heaven, make Your name real in my life as it is in heaven. Please honor Yourself by the way You enable me to live.

We bring honor to the name when we speak truth, because Yahweh is a God of truth. We bring honor to the name when we seek justice, for Yahweh is just and loves justice. We bring honor to the name when we do mercy, for Yahweh is merciful, oh so merciful! We bring honor to the name when we are patient with sinners in the process of being redeemed, for Yahweh is slow to lose patience. We bring honor to the name when we give ourselves to the poor, to the marginalized, to the needy, for Yahweh is the God of the marginalized. We bring honor to the name when we enter one another's suffering, for Yahweh is the Suffering Servant, "a man of sorrows, and acquainted with grief" (Isaiah 53:3). We bring honor to the name when we practice hospitality toward one another and toward strangers, for Yahweh is the hospitable, the welcoming God. We bring honor to the name when we step out and share our faith with the world, for Yahweh seeks to have His name named among all of the nations. We bring honor to the name when we try to make peace, when we work at reconciliation, for Yahweh is the God of peace, the great Reconciler. We bring honor to the name when we "keep hope alive," for Yahweh holds the world in His hands. Jesus will have His way. And we bring honor to the name when we live sacrificially for the Kingdom's sake, for Yahweh's great moment of glory was on the cross, when He laid down His life for the world.

(3) Thirdly, I take up God's name in vain when I throw

it around carelessly, thoughtlessly, and flippantly. We do this when we use any of God's names to express anger, frustration or surprise. You know what I mean. But we also do this within our religious circles. We preachers may do it the most! Use the name for our own agendas. I recall with shame the times I have used the name in theological debates; I have spoken Jesus' name simply to win an argument.

"Jesus." There simply is no more precious name in all the universe. How can we say it without profound gratitude? How can we say it without humbling ourselves before Him?

In the third commandment, God tells us that God takes the name Yahweh seriously. That is putting it mildly! "For Yahweh will not leave the one unpunished who takes His name in vain" (Exodus 20:7). Why? Because the consonants and vowels are so sacred? No, because disregard for the name reveals disregard for Yahweh: Jesus says that the words that come from our lips, however unintentional, reveal the attitude of our hearts (see Luke 6:45). If we throw the name around carelessly, it reveals the carelessness of our hearts.

Because God takes the name seriously, strict Jews chose not to utter it at all. By the first century it was uttered only once a year: on Yom Kippur, the Day of Atonement, by the High Priest in the Holy of Holies. How tragic!

A friend of mine was trying to get in touch with me. He left a message on my answering machine: "Darrell, this is Chap. Here is my cell phone number. I will leave the phone on all day. Call anytime. I really want to connect." *That is why God gave the name.* "I really want to connect. I will leave the machine on all day. Here is the number: Y-H-W-H, J-E-S-U-S." Not to speak the name at all is to take the name in vain, for not to speak the name means we fail to *understand* who Yahweh is—the God who is there, with us and for us.

Negative. And now the positive.

We take up God's name with honor, in fullness, when we "call upon the name." The opposite of carelessness and flippancy is praise and prayer.

Take some time today or tomorrow and read the Psalms watching for the way the psalmists "call upon the name." Remember that behind the English title, "The LORD," is the Hebrew name Yahweh. Read the Psalm out loud using God's personal name:

Arise, O Yahweh, save me, O my God!

Psalm 3:7

Give ear to my words, O Yahweh,
Consider my groaning.

Psalm 5:1

O Yahweh, do not rebuke me in Your anger...

Psalm 6:1

Heal me, O Yahweh, for my bones are dismayed.

Psalm 6:2

...Yahweh has heard the voice of my weeping.

Psalm 6:8

I love You, O Yahweh, my strength.

Yahweh is my rock and my fortress and my deliverer,

My God, my rock in whom I take refuge....

...I call upon Yahweh, who is worthy to be praised,

And I am saved from my enemies.

...In my distress I called upon Yahweh...

Psalm 18:1–3, 6

On it goes, calling on The Name.

Just before Moses died he received, for the people of Israel, all of the blessings of their redemption. One of the blessings was this: "What great nation is there that has a god so near to it as is Yahweh our God whenever we call upon Him" (Deuteronomy 4:7). Of course Yahweh is near; that is what the name means: "I am there with you and for you, all that I am I am with you and for you." Yahweh always acts in a way that hallows this name; God never acts in ways that go against this name. "I am there with you and for you."

Calling on the name of Yahweh turns out to be the highest form of honor we can give, higher than praise. For when I call on the name, I am acknowledging that Yahweh is greater than I, and that I cannot make it without Jesus. The reverse is also true. Never calling on the name is the greatest insult. It says, "I can make it without Yahweh, without Jesus."

Now you can see why I thought of subtitling this chapter, "Something Worse than Profanity." Joy Davidman puts it best: "Many church-goers think of the third commandment as meant primarily to forbid casual profanity. Yet casual profanity is perhaps the least of our offenses against it. We commit the ultimate blasphemy by not calling upon God at all."[12]

The ultimate blasphemy? Yes, because not calling upon God says we do not need God no matter what the name is.

"I Am Yahweh, your God, who brought you out of slavery.
I am Yeshua your Savior who claims you for My own.
I give you My Name.
Do not let it be in vain."

---

12 Davidman, op.cit., 44.

EXODUS 20:8

"Remember the Sabbath day, to keep it holy."

6 + 1:
RHYTHM OF WHOLENESS

The crucial line of the Ten Commandments is not a commandment. The crucial line of the Ten Commandments is the opening
sentence, "the preamble," as some call it, or "the prologue," as
others call it. The crucial line of the Ten Commandments is
a declaration of fact—a great declaration of a great fact. Lose
touch with this declaration and we miss the whole point of the
commandments. Lose touch with the declaration and the Law,
the good Law, becomes a crushing burden. The Ten Commandments begin not with a commandment but with a declaration,
an affirmation:

> "I am Yahweh your God, who brought you out of the land of
> Egypt, out of the house of slavery."
>
> Exodus 20:2

"I am Yahweh." I, the Lawgiver, am the God who has a name.
My name means "I am the One who is there with you and for you."

"I am Yahweh your God." The phrase, "your God," is the language of covenant—the language of covenant relationship. "Your God." The point being, the Lawgiver establishes a relationship with us *before* speaking the commandments. Which means that keeping the Law is not the basis of the relationship. Keeping the Law is the way we enter into deeper intimacy with Yahweh, as we will see today. But keeping the Law is not the basis of the relationship. "'I am your God...' before you hear what I am commanding you to do."

"I am Yahweh your God, who brought you out of the house of slavery." The Lawgiver is the Liberator. The God who speaks the Law is the God who comes to set us free. The God who speaks the Law sees our bondage, hears our cry for release, feels our suffering, and comes down to set us free. Free *from*, free for: from oppression and addiction, for relationship and wholeness. The God whose name is Yahweh snatched the Hebrew slaves *from* captivity in Egypt, *in order to* bring them into relationship with Himself and with each other in Him.

Why then the commandments? Why the Law? To protect and enhance that freedom! To protect and enhance the full enjoyment of that freedom! Yahweh speaks the Ten Commandments to guard and nurture a new quality of life for which He set us free.

Unless we get this, unless we embrace this fact about the Law, we probably will not do what it takes to obey the commandments.

In the first commandment, Yahweh sets us free *from* lesser gods who always turn out to be non-gods. In the first commandment, God tells us something about ourselves which we would *never* have figured out on our own. We were made *for* Yahweh. We were made *by* Yahweh *for* Yahweh. Our finite hearts can only be satisfied by the Infinite God. That is what makes us so significant: only the Infinite God can fill us and fulfill us. So to keep us from ruining our lives, God commands us, "You shall have no other gods before Me."

In the second commandment, Yahweh sets us free *from* false concepts of God. Yahweh wants to be known as Yahweh really is, undistorted by any of our human-made images. So to keep us from ruining our lives, God commands us, "You shall not make for yourself an image [of Me], or any likeness [of Me]. Only I can tell you who I am, which I have done in Jesus of Nazareth—My image of Myself."

In the third commandment, Yahweh sets us free to call upon His name. The Living and Holy God gives us the freedom to address God by God's personal name, to enter into a relationship on a first-name basis. Understandably, God does not want to see the gift of the name being wasted. So to keep us from cheating ourselves, and thereby ruining our lives, God commands us, "You shall not take the name of Yahweh your God in vain."

In the fourth commandment, Yahweh sets us free from one of the biggest obstacles to intimacy: "rat-race-ness." In the fourth commandment, our Maker and Jealous Lover sets us free from "rat-race-ness" for "human-race-ness." The fourth commandment frees us from becoming, as they say, "human doings" instead of "human beings."

"Remember the Sabbath day, to keep it holy. Six days you shall labor and do all your work, but the seventh day is a Sabbath of Yahweh your God; in it you shall not do any work, you or your son or your daughter, your male or your female servant or your cattle or your sojourner who stays with you. For in six days

Yahweh made the heavens and the earth, the sea and all that
is in them, and rested on the seventh day; therefore Yahweh
blessed the Sabbath day and made it holy."

Exodus 20:8–11

According to the prophets—especially the three major ones,
Isaiah, Jeremiah, and Ezekiel—there is no clearer indication that
we are actually living in the new freedom than when we obey
the fourth commandment. Or to put it differently, there is no
clearer indication that we are obeying the first commandment,
"You shall have no other gods before Me," than that we obey the
fourth commandment, "Remember the Sabbath day, to keep it
holy." According to the prophets, especially Isaiah, keeping the
fourth commandment is one of the best ways to move toward
keeping the first commandment (see Isaiah 30:15–18; 58:13–14).

Why? Because *one of the clearest indications of what we value is
how we spend our time.* How we spend our time is an even clearer
indication of who or what our true God is than the way we spend
our money. We all have the same amount of time *allocated* to
us: sixty minutes an hour, twenty-four hours a day, seven days
a week. How we spend our time reveals our true allegiances.

"Remember the Sabbath day, to keep it holy. Six days you shall
labor and do all your work, but the seventh day is a Sabbath of
Yahweh your God."

Exodus 20:8–10a

Sabbath keepers are an increasingly rare bird in our time.
They were rare birds in Moses' time. Indeed, there were none
until Moses came down the mountain with the good Law of the

good God. But, as rare as Sabbath keepers are, you can spot them pretty quickly. They stand out in the rat-race; they stand out in the midst of all of the hype and anxiety and frantic weariness.

Why?

As is the case in each of the Ten Commandments, in the fourth commandment the Lawgiver, who is our Maker, lets us in on who we are as human beings. Here we have another form of "The Manufacturer's Specifications." The fourth commandment is not an imposition on the human species, it is an exposition of who we were called to be.

The fourth commandment tells us two things about ourselves:

(1) First, the Living God *has built into us a particular rhythm of time.* It is the so-called "Sabbatical rhythm": six plus one. Six plus one is built into the very fabric of our bodies, into the very fabric of our psyches and into our souls. Six days of work: not three, not five, but six. We were made to be creative and productive. One day of rest: not two, not four, but one. Six plus one (six days of work, one day of rest) is the "bio-rhythm" of the human species. We were not created to handle pressure, tension, and stress every day, day in and day out. We will burn out. Nor were we created for constant leisure. We will "bore-out." We are "sabbatical creatures," creatures who work, and work hard; but who must stop every seventh day to rest, reflect and worship. To violate this rhythm is to violate our essential nature; it is to do violence to God's good creation.

Notice, by the way, how much of life is governed by the "sabbatical rhythm of time." Not only do we human beings need sabbatical rest, the animals need it also. Later on in Exodus we read: "Six days you are to do your work, but on the seventh day you shall cease from labor in order that your ox and your donkey may rest..." (Exodus 23:12). Even the land needs rest. Every seventh year Israel was to let the fields lie fallow (Exodus 23:10).

God has built into the whole universe the six plus one rhythm. The fourth commandment simply calls us to "get with the program." "Obey the rhythm." "Obey the Manufacturer's specifications: Runs Best on 6 + 1."

In the fourth commandment our Maker is saying, "I am revealing a mystery, one you would never have figured out on your own. You are built in such a way that wholeness is experienced in six plus one."

(2) Second, we learn in the fourth commandment that our ultimate worth as human beings is not found in our work, however worthy our work might be. Our ultimate worth is found in a Person, in relationship with the Living God.

So, in order to keep us from ruining our lives by idolizing our work, the Living God calls us to stop every seventh day. God commands us to stop. To stop and get in touch again with our eternal value, to regain eternal perspective, to re-root our lives in the eternal life of our Maker and Jealous Lover of our souls. God commands us to stop, and for one day to shift the focus off of ourselves and our work, onto Yahweh and His work; without which work, our work does not happen (see Psalm 92:4).

It is crucial that we notice how the commandment is structured. The emphasis of the fourth commandment is not, "You shall not work on the Sabbath." The emphasis is on, "You shall remember the Sabbath day to keep it holy." Not working on the Sabbath day is the means to a greater end—keeping the day holy. "Holy." "Holy" is what God is. "Holy" is God's essential nature. "Holy" means "separate from," "other than," "unique," "different." To keep the Sabbath holy means to keep it as a separate day, a unique day, a different day—a day set aside for the Holy God.

Yes, the commandment calls us to stop working every seventh day. But the Sabbath is not just "a day off." We can take a day off and not experience the Sabbath.[1] We are commanded to stop in order to intentionally worship and enjoy God in an undistracted way. For our worth—our significance, our identity—is not found in our work or ministry. Our worth—our significance, our identity—is found in a Person.

So, out of mercy and grace, the Person, our Maker and Redeemer, commands us to set aside one day out of seven for Him. Every day is, of course, God's. The fourth commandment is not drawing a line between the religious and the secular or the sacred and the profane. All days are God's days. But the Sabbath is a special day—a day set aside solely for the Living God. "A Sabbath of Yahweh your God." "My day." "Our day." "The day we go deeper."

The question is how? How do we keep the Sabbath holy?

Before answering that question, this is as good a place as any to address the *when* question. When do we observe the Sabbath? Specifically, why do most Christians celebrate the Sabbath on Sunday, the first day of the week, instead of on Saturday, the seventh day of the week?

We need to go back and recall why Israel celebrated the Sabbath on the seventh day. There are two reasons, one found in the Exodus form of the fourth commandment, the other found in the Deuteronomy form of the commandment.

In Exodus 20:11, Israel affirms that Yahweh made the heaven, the earth and the sea in six days; and then rested on the seventh.

---

1 Eugene Peterson, *Working the Angles* (Grand Rapids: Eerdmans, 1987), 48.

God resting is God's way of declaring that the work of creating the universe is finished. "Now is the time to enjoy it." So, on the Sabbath, Israel commemorated what God did as Creator; and on the Sabbath Israel entered into the Creator's own satisfaction with creation.

In Deuteronomy, Israel affirms that Yahweh the Creator is also the One who redeemed Israel: "You shall remember that you were a slave in the land of Egypt, and Yahweh [The LORD] your God brought you out of there by a mighty hand and by an outstretched arm; therefore Yahweh your God commanded you to observe the Sabbath day" (Deuteronomy 5:15). So, on the Sabbath, Israel also commemorated what God did as Redeemer—how God rescued His people from bondage.

The Sabbath, therefore, commemorates (1) what God did as *Creator*, and (2) what God did as *Redeemer*.

What does this have to do with the shift from Saturday to Sunday? Everything! On the first day of the week, Jesus of Nazareth, *Yeshua*—Yahweh to the Rescue—rose from the grave.

What does the resurrection mean?

(1) It means that *the ultimate redemption has been achieved*. The new exodus has taken place. Jesus has fought the enemies of humanity and won! That hideous alliance—of sin and death and the demonic—which holds humanity in bondage, had unleashed all of its fury on Jesus at the cross. But on the first day of the week, Jesus broke out of the grave. He had defeated the enemies and rescued His people. Sin had been condemned. The devil had lost his weapon. Death had lost its sting. The Redeemer had won!

(2) But the resurrection means even more. Easter morning was the first day not only of a new week, but of a new creation. In Jesus' resurrection, God had begun a new creation which can

never be destroyed by sin, death, or the demonic. Jesus Himself is the "first-born" (Colossians 1:18) of that new creation. I like how G. K. Chesterton puts it: On the first day of the week, "the friends of Christ coming at daybreak to the place found the grave empty and the stone rolled away. In varying ways, they realized the new wonder. But even they hardly realized that the world had died in the night. What they were looking at was the first day of a new creation, with a new heaven and a new earth; and in a semblance of the gardener, God walked again in the garden, in the cool, not the evening, but the dawn."[2] I think I have quoted those words in every Easter sermon I have preached!

The first day of the week, therefore, took on greater significance than the seventh. More important than the seventh day of the old creation is the first day of the new creation.

So the Church slowly moved the Sabbath from Saturday to Sunday. On the first day of the week we celebrate what God has done as Redeemer, but now it is God's final act of redemption through the blood of Jesus the Lamb. And we celebrate what God has done as Creator, but now it's God's new act of creation in the resurrected Nazarene.[3]

"Remember the Sabbath to *keep* it holy." Not "remember the Sabbath to *make* it holy." We can make nothing holy. The Sabbath already is holy. We keep the day holy because it already is. God has made it holy.

Why? Why has God established a special day?

---

2 G. K. Chesterton, *The Everlasting Man* (San Francisco: Ignatius Press, 1993), 214.
3 See Paul K. Jewett, *The Lord's Day: A Theological Guide to the Christian Day of Worship*.

Go back way before the giving of the Law. Go back to the beginning. In the first chapter of Genesis we see God at work. We see God in boundless energy and creativity calling forth light and stars and fruit trees and sea monsters and men and women. But, although God is actively involved in this work, God is not totally absorbed in it. That is, God still remains above it, beyond it, other than it. There is more to God than what we see in God working. God has more of Himself to give beyond all He gives in the six days of creation. There is something of God He can only give on the Sabbath.

So how? How do we keep the Sabbath holy? Is it even possible in a world that has long ago reduced the Lord's Day to just another day to keep up the rat race?

One sure way *not* to keep it is by legislating it. That is what the rabbis of the first century did. By the time Jesus came on the scene, the rabbis had come up with one thousand five hundred and twenty-one things one could not do on Sabbath. There is a Jewish document called the *Mishnah*, a collection of all the authoritative teaching of the rabbis. In the book, *Sabbat*, we read of the following thirty-nine things one could not do:

> The main tasks prohibited are forty save one: he who sows and plows and reaps and binds; he who threshes and winnows and fans; he who sifts and kneads and bakes; he who shears wool and bleaches it and combs and dyes and spins; he who weaves and draws and twists and separates two threads; he who ties and unties a knot and sews two stitches and tears apart to sew two stitches; he who hunts and kills and skins a gazelle; he who salts it and dresses its skin and scrapes and cuts it; he who writes two letters and rubs out again to write two letters; he who

builds and pulls down; he who lights a fire and puts it out; he who strikes with a hammer; he who carries from one place to another. These are the main tasks, forty save one.

Sabbat 7, 2

In the *Mishnah* book, *Beza*, we have yet another list of prohibited activities:

On account of the following activities (one incurs guilt on the Sabbath or feasts) by reason of the Sabbath rest: one is not to climb a tree, nor ride on an animal, nor swim in water, nor clap the hands, nor slap the hips, nor dance. On account of the following activities one incurs guilt even though they are legitimate as such: one is not to administer justice, nor become engaged to woman, nor go through the ceremony of casting off the shoe (in refusing Levirate marriage), nor contract Levirate marriage. On account of the following activities one incurs guilt even though they are based on a commandment: one is not to sanctify anything, nor make an evaluation, nor bring under the ban, nor separate heave offerings and tithes.

Beza 5, 2

Even these two lists do not cover all of the prohibitions. One could not heal a sick person on the Sabbath, unless the person was in immediate danger of dying. The rabbis even spelled out the quantities which could be lawfully carried on the Sabbath:

He is guilty who carries enough wine for the mixing of a cup, enough milk for a sip, honey sufficient to put on a wound. [He is guilty] who carries enough cord to make a handle for a basket or enough ink to write two letters.

Sabbat 8:1–4

In defense of the rabbis we need to recall their motive for making these lists. They wanted to guarantee obedience to the Law. The one thousand five hundred and twenty-one prohibitions were, in their minds, "a fence" which was "designed to prevent any possibility of doing any work on the Sabbath."[4]

You can see why Jesus got in such trouble with the religious authorities. Jesus was always breaking the rules, especially about healing people not in danger of death. Jesus did not break the fourth commandment, just the human-made rules piled on the commandment (see Mark 2:23–3:6; Luke 13:10–16; 14:1–6; John 5:1–18; 9:13–17; Matthew 12:1–7).

Jesus' defense of His actions leads us to the proper way to keep the Sabbath holy. Jesus says: "The Sabbath was made for humankind, and not humankind for the Sabbath" (Mark 2:27). That is, the real needs of men and women are of greater value than endless religious regulations. God has given us the Sabbath as a gift, a gift to enhance life not drain it. Then Jesus goes further and says: "Consequently, the Son of Man [Jesus' favorite way of referring to Himself] is Lord even of the Sabbath" (Mark 2:28).

Jesus claims to be the One who instituted the Sabbath in the first place! He set people free from the one thousand five hundred and twenty-one rules, to enjoy the day, to respond to human need, to do good, to do mercy and to heal broken lives.

---

4 Eduard Lohse, "sabbaton", *Theological Dictionary of the New Testament. Vol. VII.* (Grand Rapids: Eerdmans, 1971), 13.

The Lord of the Sabbath comes to earth to rescue the Sabbath from legalism.

The rabbis focused on the wrong part of the fourth commandment: "You shall not work." That is not where God puts the focus. They should have focused on making the Sabbath a day to *be with* God, the day to *enter into deeper communion* with God. If they had focused on the Lord of the Sabbath Himself, they would not have needed the one thousand five hundred and twenty-one rules.

So, how do we keep the Sabbath holy in our time?

Five verbs:

DESIRE. Desire the Sabbath rest. Desire the rest that God desires to give us when we stop. That is, desire the part of God that is only received and experienced when we stop. Desire the Lord of the Sabbath Himself.

DECIDE. Decide to obey the commandments. They are not the "Ten Suggestions." They are commandments. Decide to obey. That is, decide to trust the Lord of the Sabbath. Does He know what He is talking about? Is God right when God tells me my worth and significance and identity are not found in my work? Is God right when God tells me God has more of God's self to give me on the Sabbath? That is, is God smarter than me? Dallas Willard says that we will never really live out our affirmation, "Jesus is Lord," until we can say, "Jesus is smart."[5] Decide that the Lord of the Sabbath is smart.

I am not saying that obedience will then be easy. It will not. Given where the world is, it will be very difficult. What helps is

---

5 Dallas Willard, *The Divine Conspiracy: Rediscovering Our Hidden Life in God* (HarperSanFrancisco, 1998), 95.

realizing that Israel had difficulty all of her history, for none of the peoples around her observed the Sabbath. The first Christians found even greater difficulty. No one in Rome set aside one day out of seven to be with the Living God. Decide. Decide to "march to the beat of a different drummer." Decide that the God who comes to us in Jesus is wanting our best in commanding us to keep the Sabbath holy.

Early in my walk with Jesus Christ, and then early in my ministry, I decided to obey the fourth commandment. In my case, the Sabbath had to be on Monday. I used to be intimidated when I heard older pastors or elders say, "Well I haven't had a Sabbath for months," implying they were more dedicated to the cause than I. But I learned early on to simply silently pray for them: "Lord forgive them for their disobedience and arrogance." None of us is so important that we cannot obey the inherent rhythm of time. Indeed, all of us are too important not to obey the rhythm!

Decide to obey.

CHANGE. Change the routines. I must restructure my activities and chores so that I can set aside the day with the great Lover of my soul. If I have so many commitments that I cannot change the routine, then I can be sure that at least one of them is not the will of God for my life. For God will not lead us into so many commitments that we can no longer enter into the Holy day. Re-evaluate the commitments. Change the routines to make it possible to obey.[6]

SEEK. Seek to be with Yahweh. We are to seek God every day. But on the Sabbath we do so more intentionally. David says:

---

6 See Marva Dawn, *Keeping The Sabbath Wholly* (Grand Rapids: Eerdmans, 1989).

"Seek Yahweh and His strength; Seek His face continually" (1 Chronicles 16:11). Isaiah says: "Seek Yahweh while He may be found.; Call upon Him while He is near" (Isaiah 55:6). God makes wonderful promises to seekers: "And you will seek Me and you will find Me, when you search for Me with all your heart" (Jeremiah 29:13). David told his son Solomon: "If you seek Him, He will let you find Him" (1 Chronicles 28:9).

Acts of mercy, by the way, do not get in the way of seeking God on the Sabbath. For as Jesus tells us, we meet Him in the hungry, the thirsty, the stranger who needs a home, the naked, the sick (Matthew 25:31–46).

The Living God finds great joy in our intentional seeking. For our seeking God is a response to God seeking us! Jesus told the woman at the well: "But an hour is coming, and now is, when the true worshipers shall worship the Father in spirit and truth; for such people the Father seeks to be His worshipers" (John 4:23).

Desire, decide, change, seek.

CELEBRATE. Do whatever it takes to celebrate what the Creator has done, to celebrate what the Redeemer has done. Israel called the Sabbath a "feast," a day of rejoicing. Find creative ways to make the day a festive day. Put flowers on the table. Bring out the brightest tablecloth. Light candles. Sing a song. Hang banners. Enjoy meals with friends.[7] If your children or neighbors ask, "Why are you acting like it is a holiday?" Say, "Because our Lord rose from the grave on Sunday, and every Sunday is Christmas, every Sunday is Easter; we are celebrating our salvation and the beginning of the new creation."

---

7 See Wayne Muller, *Sabbath: Finding Rest, Renewal, And Delight In Our Busy Lives* (New York: Bantam Books, 1999).

Celebrate. I think it is the key for recapturing the Sabbath. The post-Christian world will not be won by coercion, or by legislation, or by guilt-tripping. People will choose to enter into the gift of the Sabbath when they see believers really enjoying it...enjoying the Lord of the Sabbath. Joy Davidman observed: "The ancient Romans, their own religion long since dwindled to spiritless and skeptical routine, suspected the Christians of perpetuating obscene orgies on their Sabbath—on the grounds that Christians obviously enjoyed the Sabbath so much!"[8] Would that the church in our time had such a reputation!

Celebration on the Sabbath does not negate weeping. Keeping the Sabbath holy does not ignore the brokenness of life. But the Sabbath reminds us of Yahweh's great victory over our brokenness at the cross and through the empty tomb. And the Sabbath points us to the final re-creation of life. As Paul Jewett put it, the Sabbath is "...a sign that God has taken our lives out of our own hands and put them in his hands."[9]

If Israel rejoiced in the desert over her salvation from Egypt, how much more can we rejoice over our greater salvation from sin, death and evil in Jesus. If Israel celebrated God's creation of the world, how much more can we celebrate God's re-creation of the world in Jesus. In Jesus' death and resurrection, God has won the victory over powers greater than Pharaoh; God has won the victory over all that threatens to undo us.

Desire the Sabbath, *decide* to obey the command, *change* the routine, *seek* the Lord of the Sabbath, and *celebrate* God's mighty deeds in Jesus Christ.

---

8 Davidman, op.cit., 55.
9 Jewett, op.cit., p.99.

I conclude with what a puritan pastor—yes, a puritan!—wrote about the gift God is giving us in the fourth commandment:

Hail thou that art highly favoured of God,
Thou golden spot of the week,
Thou marker-day of souls,
Thou daybreak of eternal brightness,
Thou queen of days.
The Lord be with thee,
Blessed art thou among days.

Oh how do men and women
Flutter up and down on weekdays,
As the dove on the waters,
And can find no rest for their souls,
Till they come to thee their ark,
Till thou put forth thy hand,
And take them in!

Oh how they sit under thy shadow
With great delight,
And find thy faith sweet to their taste!

Oh the mounting of mind,
The ravishing happiness of heart,
The solace of soul,
Which on thee they enjoy
In the blessed Savior![10]

---

10 George Swinnock, quoted by J.I. Paker in *A Quest for Godliness: The Puritan Vision of the Christian Life* (Crossway Books; Wheaton, Ill. 1990), 204.

EXODUS 2:12

"Honor your father and your mother,
that your days may be prolonged."

HONORING MOM AND DAD:
THE WAY SOCIETY GETS BLESSED

As the Apostle Paul points out in his letter to the Ephesians (6:2), the fifth commandment, "Honor your father and your mother," is the first of the Ten Commandments with a promise, "that your days may be prolonged."

A friend of mine, Avis Dahlen, had just celebrated her mother's one-hundredth birthday. In a note to me, Avis said, "Mom must have honored her father and her mother."

As I tried to demonstrate, there is a sense in which the Ten Commandments are also the Ten Promises. Given who the Lawgiver is, given who the commandment commander is, each commandment, in the final analysis, turns out to be a promise. Commandment one: "You shall have no other gods before Me." Given who Yahweh is, i.e. the only true God, and given Yahweh's zealous passion for our wholeness, the commandment is ultimately a promise: one day no other gods will come between us and the Living God.

But the fifth commandment, which is ultimately a promise, is the one commandment that comes with an explicit promise: "…that your days may be prolonged in the land Yahweh your God gives you." In Deuteronomy 5, the second telling of the Law, the promise is expanded: "That your days may be prolonged, and that it may go well with you on the land which Yahweh your God gives you."

Before we try to unpack the meaning of the fifth commandment, it is important to observe the commandment's place in the Law.

Tradition has it that Moses comes down off Mt. Sinai with the Ten Commandments written on two stone tablets (Exodus 24:12; 31:18). Although the tradition nowhere tells us which commandments were written on which tablet, it is clear that the ten belong in two categories: in what we can call the *vertical* and the *horizontal*. The first group of commandments deals with our *vertical* relationship with the Living God; the second group deals with our *horizontal* relationship with the people around us. The first group was likely etched on the first stone tablet, the second group on the second stone tablet. Thus, when Jesus was asked, "What is the greatest commandment?" He said, "The foremost is, 'and you shall love Yahweh your God with all your heart, and with all your soul and with all your mind, and with all your strength.' And the second is this, 'You shall love your neighbor as yourself'" (Mark 12:28–31). First tablet—love God. Second tablet—love your neighbor.

We have made our way through the first tablet, through commandments one to four, teaching us how to love God. Now we begin making our way through the second tablet, through commandments five to ten, teaching us how to love our neighbors.

The fifth commandment, "Honor your father and your mother," stands at the top of the second tablet. That is, it stands at the turning point from the vertical to the horizontal, at the place where the vertical and horizontal intersect. As the Lawgiver moves from our relationship with Him to our relationship with our neighbors, God begins with the first relationship we all experience, the relationship with parents. "I am Yahweh your God, who has acted to free you from bondage. Honor your father and your mother, that your days may be prolonged, that it may go well with you."

As we grapple with this pivotal commandment, I am very much aware of three sets of people. The first set is my father and mother and me; my father-in-law and mother-in-law and me; Sharon and our four children and my daughter-in-law and me; and all the "stuff" that is going on in those relationships. The second set of people is those who have shared with me the pain that exists between them and their parents, or between them and their children.[1] The third set of people is Jesus and His earthly parents; *Y'shua*, Yahweh-to-the-Rescue, and His biological mother, Mary, and His adoptive father, Joseph. I have this third set in mind because in it we see the Giver of the Law Himself, now incarnated in our flesh, living out His own commandments. We see in Jesus' relationship with Mary and Joseph the full implications of the fifth commandment.

"Honor your father and your mother that your days may be prolonged, and that it may go well with you."

---

1 I do not know how to address some of the horrific stories I have heard about parental abuse. I do have such needs in my heart as I develop this chapter, but am keenly aware of how unprepared I am to minister deep healing.

What is the Living God getting at in this commandment?

As I have been emphasizing in this book, the Giver of the Law is the Creator. Yahweh is the One who made us. In each of the commandments, the Creator is telling us something about ourselves. In the first four commandments God reveals things about ourselves that we would have never figured out on our own. I was going to say that in the fifth commandment God reveals something we would have figured out on our own. But given how human societies drift on this matter, I am not going to say that. For, apparently, we have not and do not get it on our own. We need this commandment.

In the fifth commandment, the Lawgiver, the Creator, is the master sociologist. As the master sociologist, Yahweh reveals how societies go together. Yahweh reveals that at the center of our corporate life is the family. The family is the basic building block of society. The family is the thread that keeps the fabric of our corporate life united and strong. As the family goes, so goes a society. A nation that wants to be vital and strong must protect and nurture the family.

Do we not see this in traditional Asian societies? There are many reasons for their stability and longevity; but chief among them is the high regard for the family, and especially the honoring of parents and grandparents. Yet, as many of you from Asian families tell us, that strength can also become abusive.

Clearly, the fifth commandment explicitly speaks a challenging word to sons and daughters. But it also implicitly speaks a challenging word to fathers and mothers. Unless fathers and mothers hear and heed this word, the fifth commandment, meant to nurture freedom, becomes an oppressive yoke on the shoulders of sons and daughters.

So, let us first listen to what the commandment says to children, children of all ages; and then let us listen to what God says to parents and grandparents.

1. God's message to sons and daughters is bound up in that word "honor."

What does it mean to "honor" one's parents? The Hebrew word carries a wide range of meanings. Its basic root means "to be burdensome," "to make heavy or weighty." It is the verb form of the noun "glory." The "glory of God" means the "weightiness of God's self-manifestation."[2]

Three particular nuances of the word "honor" are developed in the Scripture in reference to our relationship with our parents.

(A) First, to "honor" our parents means to respect them. It means to feel the weightiness of their position.[3] In the book of Leviticus, the word "honor" is replaced by the word "fear" or "reverence." There God says, "Every one of you shall reverence his mother and his father" (Leviticus 19:3). We are to recognize the weight—the load—parents carry. God has entrusted to parents the weighty responsibility of taking care of God's vulnerable creatures. Parents carry the weight of shaping our values, forming our self-image, building the basis of our self-worth; helping us develop the basis of our significance and security; giving us our initial ideas about who God is! That is a huge burden! And remember—every parent enters this responsibility as a rookie!

---

2 Gerhard von Rad, "doxa", *Theological Dictionary of the New Testament Vol.I.* (Grand Rapids: Eerdmans, 1964), 239.
3 I owe this to Earl Palmer in the aforementioned sermon.

This respect for parents' position translates into everyday terms as respecting their advice, their discipline, and their guidance. So we read over and over again in the book of Proverbs sayings like these:

> A wise son accepts his father's discipline,
> But a scoffer does not listen to rebuke.
>
> Proverbs 13:1

> Listen to your father who begot you, and do not despise your mother when she is old.
>
> Proverbs 23:22

> He who curses his father or his mother,
> His lamp will go out in time of darkness.
>
> Proverbs 20:20

"Honor" first of all means respect.

Such respect is, of course, not absolute. That is, children (especially as they grow older) are to weigh their parents' input. They are to put their parents' input on a scale and weigh it against God's input. You see, sons and daughters are also called to respect the Living God. They are also called to honor God, to obey the first commandment: "You shall have no other gods before Me." (Not even parents!) So Jesus, who definitely upholds the fifth commandment, also says to us: "The one who loves father or mother more than Me is not worthy of Me; and the one who loves son or daughter more than Me is not worthy of Me..." (Matthew 10:37). We are to honor our parents in the context of honoring Jesus as Lord. As Lord of my life, Jesus now has the last word—over my decisions about my life's work, over my values, over my goals in life, over my way of life, over my self-perception. If one's parents do not accept the Lordship of Jesus, a child who does is put in a painful crunch. In such a case, parents may get hurt—for the child is called to respect the input of her/his Lord over the input of her/his parents. Absolute respect is given only to the Lord Himself.

The first meaning of "honor" is respect.

(B) To honor our parents, secondly, means to obey them.

We read in Proverbs: "My son, observe the commandment of your father, and do not forsake the teaching of your mother; bind them continually on your heart; tie them around your neck" (Proverbs 6:20–21). The Apostle Paul, commenting on the fifth commandment, writes: "Children, obey your parents in the Lord, for this is right" (Ephesians 6:1).

Obeying our parents pleases God because it honors God's ordering of human life. God has placed parents in a place of authority on God's behalf. The Apostle Paul says in Romans that disobeying parents is an expression of the fallen world: "And just as they did not see fit to acknowledge God any longer, God gave them over to a depraved mind, to do those things which were not proper, being filled with all unrighteousness, wickedness, greed, evil; full of envy, murder, strife, deceit, malice; they are gossips, slanderers, haters of God, insolent, arrogant, boastful, inventors of evil, disobedient to parents..." (Romans 1:28–30). And Paul tells Timothy that disobedience to parents is one of the signs of the end times: "But realize this, that in the last days difficult times will come. For people will be lovers of self, lovers of money, boastful, arrogant, revilers, disobedient to parents, ungrateful, unholy..." (2 Timothy 3:1–2).

The Manufacturer is telling us that life goes better if sons and daughters obey the Lord of Life by obeying their fathers and mothers.

Again, such obedience is not absolute. As children grow toward adulthood they develop other relationships, which also call for obedience. The obligations of those relationships may at times conflict with the requests of parents.

One such relationship is marriage. When a son marries, he owes greater allegiance to his wife than his parents. In Genesis we read: "A man shall leave his mother and father and cleave unto his wife, and the two shall become one flesh" (Genesis 2:24). Marriage calls one to a new loyalty, a loyalty that is stronger than the ties of blood.

Another relationship that calls for loyalty and obedience is the child's relationship with the Living God. Absolute obedience can be given only to God in Jesus Christ. Another way of saying this is that the first commandment is always the first: "You shall have no other gods before Me."

This realization helps check the potential dangers of the so-called "chain of command" teaching. Some Bible teachers argue that God communicates His will to us through lines of authority. In particular, God communicates His will to sons and daughters through their parents. Many young adults go through great inner turmoil because of abuses of that concept, thinking that they must never act contrary to their parents' wishes, because their parents' wishes are equal to God's wishes. That might be true if the parents are perfectly committed to God's will—if they are totally open to the leading of the Holy Spirit. But what parent can make that claim? Besides, there comes a time when the child is directly accountable to God. The child is then obligated to weigh the parents' will against what he/she knows to be God's will.

We see this tension in the life of the incarnate Lawgiver. As a young boy, Jesus did submit Himself to His parents' direction and leadership. However, when He was twelve years old He left a family gathering to spend time in the Temple talking with the teachers. His parents looked all over for Him. When they found Him, His mother said to Him: "Child, why have you treated us this way? Behold, your father and I have been anxiously looking for You." Jesus' responses: "Why is it that you were looking for Me? Did you not know that I had to be in My Father's house?" (Luke 2:48–49). Jesus' relationship to His Heavenly Father took precedence over His relationship to Joseph and Mary. Yet we should note that after Luke records that story, he tells us that Jesus did return to Nazareth and "continued in subjection to them" (Luke 2:51). Although He knew He had to obey the heavenly Father first, He nonetheless did so with respect for His earthly parents.

We honor our parents by respecting them; we honor our parents by obeying them.

(C) To honor our parents, thirdly, means to care for them, to accept the weight of their needs. Such care takes on different forms at different times in our lives.

For instance, as a number of scholars have suggested, while parents are still able to take care of themselves, we care by protecting their reputations, by covering up their faults. There is a very touching story in the book of Genesis that illustrates such care. The great flood had subsided, and Noah and his family had settled on the land again. One day Noah was apparently in a celebrating mood. He began to drink the wine from his newly planted vineyard. He drank so much he got terribly drunk. One of Noah's sons found him lying in his tent stark naked. Then we are told that Noah's other sons took a garment, "laid it upon their shoulders and walked backward [into the tent] and covered the nakedness of their father..." (Genesis 9:23). We can care for our parents by not shaming them—by keeping their faults within the family; or by sharing their faults only with those who can help us help them.

We can care for them by providing for their needs when they can no longer do so for themselves. Old Testament scholar Brevard Childs points out that the original situation into which God spoke the fifth commandment found parents being driven out of the home after they could no longer work.[4] How contemporary! Is this not how even our society tends to treat the aged? They are supposedly no longer useful, they add nothing to the Gross National Product, so are put on a shelf. The Creator commands us to honor and care for the elderly.

In the first century, some people used a "spiritual" justification to get around this obligation. Some rabbis taught, if a son had dedicated all of his money to God, he need not be concerned to provide for his father or mother. He could say with a clear conscience "even if I wanted to help you I can't. My money is Corban—that is, "given to God" (see Mark 7:1–13). Funny how they thought that God's work did not include loving parents! Jesus condemned that teaching for what it was: a rationalization of disobedience of God's clear command.

Our culture does the same thing. We cannot help the aged

---

4 Brevard S. Childs, *The Book of Exodus: A Critical, Theological Commentary* (Philadelphia: Westminster Press, 1974), 418.

because we, too, have dedicated our resources to a god. The god in this case is our lifestyle. We do not say it with words, but our actions say it loud and clear: "Sorry, Mom and Dad. I'd like to help you but all of my resources and time are dedicated to maintaining my lifestyle. I just can't help you."

The fifth commandment calls us to stop and think about what our parents have done for us. Look how they sacrificed their lifestyle for us, for ten to twenty years—or more, if they are still paying college bills, as someone has pointed out. Isn't it only fair that we return a decade or two of care to them? Think of how totally dependent we were on them for at least five years. We stifled their lifestyle with our dirty diapers, our messy eating habits and our crying at night. Think of all of the inconvenience we caused. Isn't it only fair to return the favor and be inconvenienced? They pushed us in our strollers for many years. Ought we not push them in their wheelchairs for many years? Paul tells Timothy to remind children and grandchildren of widows, "to put their religion into practice by caring for their own family, and so repaying their parents and grandparents, for this is pleasing to God" (see 1 Timothy 5:4). Many of you readers are no doubt having to care for your parents as though they were dependent infants. God will bless you for that; you will hear God's "Well done, good and faithful servant."

We honor our parents as we accept the "burden," the "weight" of their needs when they can no longer do for themselves.

The Lawgiver modeled this from the cross. Even as He was dying, Jesus made arrangements for his mother's needs. To the beloved disciple John, He said, in reference to Mary, "Behold your mother!" And John tells us, "And from that hour the disciple took her into his own household" (John 19:27).

A number of years ago, a cherished friend of mine, Mike Dennis, said to me, "We need an eleventh commandment: parents honor your sons and daughters." If you understand the fifth commandment rightly, it contains the eleventh commandment.

The Apostle Paul makes this clear in his letter to the Ephesians. After quoting the commandment, he writes: "And, fathers, do not provoke your children to anger; but bring them up in the discipline and instruction of the Lord" (Ephesians 6:4). And in Colossians Paul writes: "Fathers, do not exasperate your children, that they may not lose heart" (Colossians 3:21). In those verses Paul is drawing out the message to parents: "honor your sons and daughters."

2. What does it mean for parents to "honor" their children?

(A) We honor our children, first, by respecting them; by recognizing their weightiness; by respecting them as persons. Children are not extensions of the parents' ego; they are unique, separate persons. They are not something to be molded into our images, but persons created in God's image. They are not something to be possessed and manipulated, but gifts of God to be discovered and set free.

As the years go by, we parents must let our children out of the "child box," to let them become peers, to let them be different and unique. As children are called to respect their parents, so parents are called to respect their children.

(B) We honor our children, secondly, by seeking Yahweh's will for their life. What are your dreams for your children? What are you pushing and encouraging them to be and do? We "honor" them by encouraging them to discover God's will for their lives. In Proverbs we read: "Train up a child in the way he should go, even when he is old he will not depart from it" (Proverbs 22:6). Some people have taken that verse to mean: "shove your children into a certain mold and even if they rebel for a while, later on they will return to it." That attitude will crush a child's spirit. The Scripture tells us that God has made every child unique. God has given every child a unique temperament, unique gifts and unique interests. Proverbs 22:6 is literally "train up a child according to his bent and when he is old he will not depart from it."[5] Our job as parents is to discover our children's unique bents, unique characteristics, and then "train them up in their way;" i.e., train them in ways consistent with his/her uniqueness. When they discover God's unique call upon their lives they will not depart from it.

That is what is meant by bringing up a child in the "nurture and admonition" of the Lord. It means being more concerned about their relationship to the Living God in Jesus Christ than anything else; more concerned for that relationship than for their intellectual growth, their health, their material property, their social status; more concerned for them to know, love and obey Jesus Christ than be spared pain and sorrow.[6] We honor our children by seeking their independent dependence upon Jesus as Lord. When I went to college, my dad gave me a pocket Bible. In it he wrote: "Here is the story of a Man who can do more for you than your dad." My dad honored me when he let me be free

---

5 I first heard Chuck Swindoll make this point on one of his radio sermons; I checked it out and he is right.
6 Francis Foulkes, *The Letter of Paul to the Ephesians: An Introduction and Commentary*, 2nd edition, (Grand Rapids, Michigan: Eerdmans, 1989), 166.

to follow Jesus.

(C) We honor our children, thirdly, by honoring Yahweh as in our own lives. Children learn by example, by the actions of people around them. Psychologist Bernard Percy makes this point in his book, *How to Grow a Child*. The book is a collection of pieces of advice given by children to their parents. One poem makes the point clear:

> Listen my parents and you shall hear
> The voice of your child,
> That sweet little dear.
> Mom, Dad, you're an example
> Of what I'm to be,
> For I act out the actions I see.[7]

We parents can mouth our faith in God all we want; our children will know by how we act whether or not our faith is real. They see our real gods through our actions. We may tell them, "Jesus is our security; His love makes us significant." But they can tell that our security is really found in our work or in our money, or that our significance is found in success or in pleasing people. We become the mothers and fathers worthy of the place given us by the fifth commandment when we ourselves obey the first commandment, "You shall have no other gods before me."

That is, we honor our children by learning to be children ourselves; children who trust the heavenly Father, who has adopted us in Jesus Christ.

---

7 Bernard Percy, *How to Grow a Child: A Child's Advice to Parents* (Los Angeles: Price/Stern/Sloan, 1978), 30.

So, how can we respond to what God has said to us in the fifth commandment?

(1) First, we can ask God to give us grace to find new ways to honor our parents; and for parents, new ways to honor our children. Maybe we need to make a phone call this afternoon or write a letter. Maybe we need to change our attitude about the weightiness of our parents or of our children. Yahweh, please help me see them as You see them; help me enter into what you are doing in their lives.

(2) Second, we can ask God to give us grace to take steps toward healing our relationship with our parents (even if they are no longer alive on earth) or steps toward healing our relationship with our children (even if the children are no longer on earth). Maybe the prayer is, "Yahweh, give me grace to say, 'I am sorry.'" Or maybe the prayer is, "Yahweh, give me grace to say, 'I forgive you.'"

In Jesus, the Living God has revealed Himself to be the great Reconciler. God's desire is to reconcile all people to Himself. And God's desire is to reconcile people to people. Vertical reconciliation. Horizontal reconciliation. Both made possible at the cross.

At the point in the Law where the vertical and horizontal meet is the fifth commandment. Is it any surprise then that the Old Testament should end the way it does?

> "Behold, I will send you Elijah the prophet before the great and terrible day of Yahweh. And he will restore the hearts of the parents to their children, and the hearts of the children to their parents..."
>
> Malachi 4:5–6

Jesus the Messiah has fulfilled that role. In Him, the heavenly Father has reconciled Himself to the world. And in Him, earthly fathers and mothers can be reconciled to their sons and daughters. Jesus can give us grace to fulfill the fifth commandment.

And then our days will be prolonged. And then it will go well on the land.

PROTEST AGAINST INHUMANITY

During the week when He was crucified, Jesus was asked by one of the scribes—by one of the teachers of the Law—"What is the greatest commandment?" Jesus answered:

> "Hear, O Israel! Yahweh your God is one Lord; And you shall love Yahweh your God with all your heart, and with all your soul and with all your mind, and with all your strength."
>
> Mark 12:29–30

And Jesus went on to say, "The second is this, 'You shall love your neighbor as yourself.' There is no other commandment greater than these" (Mark 12:31).

Jesus sums up the whole Law under two great loves: the vertical love for the Living God, and the horizontal love for the people around us.

The apostle Paul can thus say: "Owe nothing to anyone except to love one another; for those who love their neighbor have fulfilled the law. For this, 'You shall not commit adultery, you shall not murder, you shall not steal, you shall not covet,' and if there is any other commandment, it is summed up in this saying, 'you shall love your neighbor as yourself.' Love does no wrong to a neighbor; love therefore is the fulfillment of the law" (Romans 13:8–10).

"Love is the fulfillment of the Law."

If we love God with all our being, that love will express itself in obedience to commandments one through four:

"You shall have no other gods before Me;
You shall not make any images of Me;
You shall not take the name of Yahweh your God in vain;
Remember the Sabbath day, to keep it holy."

And if we love our neighbors as we love ourselves, that love will express itself in obedience to commandments five through ten:

"Honor your father and your mother;
You shall not murder;
You shall not commit adultery;
You shall not steal;
You shall not bear false witness;
You shall not covet anything that belongs to your neighbor."

Putting it this way makes us see just how loveless our world is. Putting it this way makes us see just how loveless our own hearts are. Putting it this way makes us see our need for help— for help from outside ourselves. Understanding the Law in this way makes us realize our need for a Savior, for Someone to come and give us a new heart.

"You shall not murder."

As you no doubt know, there is much debate about the scope of this commandment. Of all ten, this one gets the most, "yes, but what about this...," kind of response. Even more than the commandment against adultery!

The great tragedy is that the Living God should even have to utter those words. The great tragedy is that creatures of the good God, made in the good image of the good God, should have to be told not to take the life of another creature. It ought to be self-evident that another person's life is sacred—however young or old, however deformed or evil. Can you feel the great grief in Yahweh's voice when it comes to speaking the sixth commandment?

"You shall not murder."

It happens every day. It happens in increasingly violent and unspeakably horrific ways. Two high school students, tired of being ostracized by the "cool crowd," master-mind the slaughter at Columbine High School in the United States. "You shall not murder." Three white men in Texas drag a black man, simply because he is black, behind a pickup truck until he dies as a shredded mess of flesh. "You shall not murder." A day trader, despairing over mounting debt, kills his family, and then goes to a stock brokerage office and mows down eight more human beings. "You shall not murder." Police officers, not wanting their errors in procedures regarding an illegal alien found out, shoot him in cold blood and then plant a gun on his bloodstained body. "You shall not murder." A six-year old boy takes a loaded gun from home, and shoots a six-year old girl at school. "You shall not murder." A gang of desperate terrorists fly passenger jets into tall buildings killing thousands. "You shall not murder."

It is going to take a whole lot more than posting the Ten Commandments on walls to overcome what Pope John Paul II called, "the culture of death."[1]

What we have in the sixth commandment is, at rock bottom, *a protest*. A protest against inhumanity. A Divine protest against inhumanity. The Creator's protest against inhumanity.

And what we have here is a call to bring our hearts to the foot of the cross, where human inhumanity is most unjustly and violently manifested; and where, ironically, it is healed.

"You shall not murder."

It is tempting for many of us to quickly say, "Yes! That's right. I've got the message." And then move on to a more relevant commandment. For the fact of the matter is, ninety-nine point nine percent of us have never murdered anyone. And we have no intention of ever doing so.

But the Lawgiver does not let us off that quickly. For Yahweh comes down from the mountain top—all the way down—and enters into the inhumanity in Person, as Jesus of Nazareth. And in His Sermon on the Mount, Jesus *deepens the protest; He extends the protest* by exposing the unresolved anger in our hearts from which the act of murder emerges.

Jesus says:

> "You have heard that the ancients were told, 'You shall not com-
> mit murder' and 'Whoever commits murder shall be liable to
> the court.' But I say to you that everyone who is angry with their
> brother or sister shall be guilty before the court; and whoever
> says to their brother or sister, 'Raca,' shall be guilty before the

---

[1] From an open air mass not long after the Columbine, Colorado shootings.

supreme court; and whoever shall say, 'You fool,' shall be guilty
enough to go into the fiery hell."

Matthew 5:21–22

"You shall not murder."

What exactly is being prohibited by the sixth commandment?
That is, what is the scope of the prohibition? Is God saying an
unqualified no to ever waging war? Is God saying no to capital
punishment? Is God protesting physician-assisted suicide, eutha-
nasia, or abortion for any reason?

Many English versions of the Bible used to translate the
commandment as, "You shall not kill." But most now do not use
the word "kill." That is because the Hebrew word used in the
Exodus text has a more specific meaning than "kill." It refers to
what we in our time call first-degree murder, the violent taking
of another person's life.

The "you" in the commandment is singular (as it is in the
other nine commandments). "You, as an individual human
being, shall not take another human being's life." The sixth
commandment is Yahweh's "yes" to life. *To take another person's
life is to speak our "no" to God's "yes."*

As is the case in each of the Ten Commandments, the Creator is here revealing something about us human beings. Every
human life, however young or old, however deformed or evil, is
sacred. Sacred because every human life, regardless of the circumstances in which it is conceived, is the work of God. *To take
the life of another human being is to destroy a work of God.*

Old Testament scholar Walther Zimmerli sharpens the point
for us. "It would be wrong to interpret this commandment as
embodying the notion of the absolute sanctity of human life.

131

What is protected is not life itself, but the life accorded a person by Yahweh."[2] Life is sacred not because it is life, but because life is a gift of God. Every human life is a gift of God. My life is a gift of God. Your life is a gift of God. Indeed, every human life is God's. Only God has the right to give it. Only God has the right to take it away.

So we can restate the sixth commandment this way: "No human being has the right to unilaterally take another human being's life; no human being has the authority or right to take the God-given life of another."

In every act of murder two claims are implicitly being made.

(1) First, the goal achieved by the act is of greater value than the God-given life of the person murdered. People kill for all kinds of reasons: to protect their status, to gain money, to get revenge, to maintain their lifestyle, or to cover up mistakes. When someone kills another person, he or she is claiming, "My status, my financial security, my lifestyle, my desire to get even, is of greater value than your life."

(2) But secondly, the act is claiming that the goal achieved is of such value that it justifies taking into one's own hands the sole prerogative of God. Since only God has the right to take away life, every act of murder is an act of idolatry. *Hubris* is the technical word: a human being presuming to exercise God's role.

This explains why King David prays the way he does in Psalm 51, the prayer David prays when, after his affair with Bathsheba and his having her husband killed, he was exposed by the prophet Nathan. David prays to God, "Against You I have sinned" (Psalm

---

2 Walther Zimmerli, *Old Testament Theology in Outline* (Atlanta: John Knox Press, 1978), 135.

51:4). He sinned against God? Wasn't his sin against Bathsheba and her vow of marriage? Wasn't his sin against Uriah, her husband, and his life? Wasn't his sin against the kingdom of Israel for his abuse of power? Yes. But fundamentally, and ultimately, all of it was against God. David had "dehumanized" Bathsheba and Uriah. And he had presumed to take the role of Yahweh into his own hands. "Against You I have sinned."

Every human being, however problematic, however evil, is the work of God. Every human being, whatever the circumstance which conceived him or her, is a creation of God. "You shall not take into your hands the right to take another person's life."

Which brings us to Jesus and His radicalizing of the sixth commandment in His Sermon on the Mount. As a former colleague of mine, K.C. Hansen, put it, "Acts do not come out of nowhere." Murder does not come out of nowhere. Acts emerge from our hearts. Jesus, therefore, makes us face what is going on in our hearts.

"You have heard the ancients were told 'You shall not murder'...but I say to you...." Jesus draws out the deeper intent of the sixth commandment. Jesus deepens, heightens and extends God's protest against inhumanity.

Jesus points to our anger against a brother or sister that is left unresolved.

And Jesus points to our sarcastic remarks. The word "Raca" is related to the word which means "empty." "You empty head!" "You idiot!" "Stupid!" It calls into question the other person's mental competence. It calls into question another person's intelligence.

And Jesus points to our insulting remarks. "You fool!" The Greek word is *morē*, from which we get the word "moron." The word is used to call into question another person's personhood, to insult another person's character. A. B. Bruce, a nineteenth century New Testament scholar, writes: "'*Raca*' expresses contempt for a person's head—you stupid! '*Morē*' expresses contempt for a person's heart—you scoundrel!"[3]

"You have heard that the ancients were told 'You shall not murder'...but I say to you...."

Notice that in Jesus' extension of the sixth commandment there is an "escalation," moving from serious to more serious acts.[4] Jesus starts with nursing our anger. Then He moves to the casual sarcastic remark, "raca." And then he moves to the deliberate insult, "You fool!"

And Jesus says there is an "escalation" of consequences, an escalating degree of judgment.[5] The nursing of anger is subject to judgment before the city council. Uttering the sarcastic remark is subject to judgment before the Supreme Court. Speaking the flagrant insult is subject to judgment in hell!

"You shall not murder"...but I say to you...." Jesus is not saying that nursing anger and uttering sarcastic and insulting words are murder. Anger is not murder. Sarcasm is not murder. Insult is not murder. Yes, as John Stott, connecting on Jesus' words, says: "Anger and insults are ugly symptoms of a desire to get rid of somebody who is in the way."[6] And, yes, sarcasm and insults

---

3 A. B. Bruce, *Synoptic Gospels* (London: Hodder and Stoughton, 1912), 107.
4 Pinchas Lapide, *The Sermon on the Mount, Utopia or Program for Action?* (Maryknoll, NY: Orbis Books, 1986), 49; Frederick Dale Bruner, *The Christbook: A Historical/Theological Commentary: Matthew 1–12* (Waco: Word Books, 1987), 175.
5 Ibid.
6 John R. W. Stott, *Christian Counter-Culture: The Message of the Sermon on the Mount* (Downers Grove: Inter-Varsity Press, 1978), 85.

are forms of "character assassination." But Jesus is not saying that anger, sarcasm, and insults *are* murder. What He is saying is that behind, beneath, and prior to the act of murder is the act of nursing anger, which spills over into sarcastic remarks and insulting words. He is telling us that homicide, the ultimate act of inhumanity, comes out of the deep reservoir of unresolved anger.

The Incarnate Lawgiver is telling us that nursing anger is just as displeasing to God as murder, just as damaging to relationships as murder, and just as deserving of judgment as murder. He is telling us that uttering casual sarcastic remarks is just as displeasing to God as murder, just as damaging to relationships as murder, and just as deserving of judgment as murder. He is telling us that verbally insulting another is just as displeasing to God as murder, just as damaging to relationships as murder, and just as deserving of judgment as murder.

Dietrich Bonhoeffer put it best in his book entitled, *The Cost of Discipleship*. The sixth commandment tells us that another person's life "is a boundary which we dare not pass." Jesus takes the protest further saying, "even anger is enough to overstep the mark, still more the casual angry word ('raca'), and most of all the deliberate insult ('You fool!')."[7]

So what do we do about the inhumanity in our hearts? "Therefore," says Jesus (Matthew 5:23). And *what* does He go on to say? He gives us a short course on how to control our temper. Right? He gives us clues on how to justify our anger. Right? He gives us new, creative ways to ignore or stuff our anger. Right?

---

7 Dietrich Bonhoeffer, *The Cost of Discipleship* (New York: Simon and Schuster, 1995), 143.

No! He gives us two examples, both from real life, teaching the one way, the only way, to deal with anger. What is it? Deal with it! Or more accurately, *deal with the person* with whom we are angry or who is angry with us.

The first example takes place in the religious realm—at church; the second takes place in the secular realm—at work.

First example:

> "So when you are offering your gift at the altar, if you remember that your brother or sister has something against you, leave your gift there before the altar and go; first be reconciled to your brother or sister, and then come and offer your gift."
>
> Matthew 5:23–24

Leave worship?

Second example:

> "Come to terms quickly with your accuser while you are on the way to court with him, or your accuser may hand you over to the judge, and the judge may hand you over to the guard, and you may be thrown into prison."
>
> Matthew 5:25–26

The key word is the adverb "quickly."

Leave worship to deal with the person who is angry with us.[8] That is how serious Jesus takes our unresolved anger. For unresolved anger turns into a cesspool of poison, out of which

---

8 At the very minimum, make the decision to deal with the person, asking God for the courage to do so ASAP.

come sarcastic results, insulting words, and eventually murder.

"Quickly," he says. Before "the sun goes down on your anger," adds Paul (Ephesians 4:26).[9] Before our hearts turn into a reservoir of bitterness and resentment.

From Jesus' extension of the protest against inhumanity, I think we can suggest four specific ways to deal with the internal violence out of which murder arises.

(1) First, realize my own heart's capacity for inhumanity. Realize that there are, in fact, times I want to get rid of the person who is in my way (Matthew 15:17–20; Jeremiah 17:9).

(2) Second, confess my inner inhumanity. Tell God what I see in myself, banking on the promise that when I do I am forgiven and cleansed (1 John 1:5–10).

(3) Third, forgive those who have inflicted their inhumanity on me. Decide to forgive. If I cannot do it, ask God to give me the grace to forgive. An unforgiving spirit will eat at me and finally express itself externally, if only in ulcers or headaches. Somewhere along the line I need to decide not to murder myself with unforgiveness. Decide to be free of the hatred, the need to get even, and the need for an apology. Forgive. A dear brother in Christ, who has been offended by another dear brother in Christ, came to me to say, "I have decided to let go of the contempt I have held in my heart."

(4) Fourth, reach out and try to reconcile. I may not succeed, but I will try. Go out of my way to reconcile hurtful relationships. It involves great risk. It all depends on how free a heart I want to have. I may be further rejected as I reach out. I may be further

---

9 I commend to you the work of Rod Wilson, President of Regent College. See his book, *Exploring Your Anger: Friend Or Foe?*.

stomped on. There have been times when I have felt like a fool, or been even further criticized. But at least the inhumanity is no longer boiling in my heart.[10]

In another of his books, *Life Together*, Dietrich Bonhoeffer describes the kind of person before whom it is safe to open the inhumanity of our hearts:

> To whom shall we make confession? According to Jesus' promise, every Christian brother can hear the confession of another. But will he understand?
>
> Anybody who lives beneath the Cross and who has discerned in the Cross of Jesus the utter wickedness of all men and of his own heart will find there is no sin that can ever be alien to him. Anybody who has once been horrified by the dreadfulness of his own sin that nailed Jesus to the Cross will no longer be horrified by even the rankest sins of a brother. Looking at the Cross of Jesus, he knows the human heart. He knows how utterly lost it is in sin and weakness, how it goes astray in the ways of sin, and he also knows that it is accepted in grace and mercy. Only the brother under the Cross can hear a confession.
>
> It is not the experience of life but experience of the Cross that makes one a worthy hearer of confessions.
>
> In daily, earnest living with the Cross of Christ the Christian loses the spirit of human censoriousness on the one hand and weak indulgence on the other, and he receives the spirit of divine severity and divine love. The death of the sinner before God and

---

10 The Giver of the Law will help us here. He really wants our hearts to be free. He will breathe His Spirit into us again, enabling us to decide and act. He will give us soul mates who help us confess and check the inhumanity stewing inside.

life that comes out of that death through grace become for him a daily reality. So he loves the brothers with the merciful love of God that leads through the death of the sinner to the life of the child of God. Who can hear our confession? He who himself lives beneath the Cross. Wherever the message concerning the Crucified is a vital, living thing, their brotherly confession will also avail.[11]

At the cross the Lawgiver breaks the power of inhumanity. How? The Lawgiver takes all of the inhumanity upon Himself. Inhumanity breeds counter-inhumanity. Violence breeds counter-violence. At the cross the chain of violence is broken. The Living God absorbs the full onslaught of human inhumanity. The cross is the protest against inhumanity taken to the limit.

Are you harboring any resentment against anyone today? Are you holding a grudge? Are you letting anger fester? Do you feel rising envy or greed? Are you bitter about how someone has treated you? Deal with it now. Now. Bring it to the Crucified One. It is the failure to deal with the violence within that makes our world so violent. We may not be able to do anything today about the violence "out there." But we can do something about the violence "in here." We can bring it to the cross.

Then maybe we can be more useful to the Savior, as He protests all forms of inhumanity.

---

11 Dietrich Bonhoeffer, *Life Together* (San Francisco: Harper & Row, 1954), 119.

EXODUS 20:14

"You shall not commit adultery."

THE MYSTERY OF
HUMAN SEXUALITY

During the 1976 campaign for the Presidency of the United States, then-candidate Jimmy Carter, a professed disciple of Jesus Christ, said some things for which he was crucified in the secular media. In July of 1976, Mr. Carter confessed to a gathering of reporters that he struggled with the sin of sexual lust. "I've looked at a lot of women with lust," he said. "I've committed adultery in my heart many times. This is something that God recognizes I will do—and I have done it—and God forgives me for it." Mr. Carter subsequently gave an interview with Playboy magazine (!) about the nature of lust and adultery, the content of which became front-page material during the rest of the campaign for President. Reporters laughed and snickered. Newspaper cartoonists had a field day.

The media's reaction to people like Jimmy Carter reveals at least two things about our society. First, it reveals our society's profound confusion about human sexuality. Modern men and women are suffering a crisis of sexual identity. Which, from a

Biblical perspective, is tragic, and yet not surprising. For, as the Apostle Paul argues in the first chapter of his letter to the Romans, when we human beings exchange the Living God for lesser gods, the first and primary consequence is sexual confusion (see Romans 1:26–27). As Earl Palmer puts it, "The first casualty in our revolution against the Creator is our sexuality."[1]

Second, the way the media responds to the Jimmy Carters of the world reveals a deep longing to understand human sexuality. Why do modern people get so worked up when the church or synagogue speaks on sex? Very few people get agitated when the church or synagogue speaks on justice, or war, or hunger, or death, or peacemaking. But speak on sex and storm clouds quickly gather. Why is this? Because we are sexual beings, intentionally created as such, and we long to understand what that means. The strong reaction of the media only reveals an awareness that something is wrong and a desire that it somehow be made right.

"You shall not commit adultery."

Because this commandment touches such a raw nerve, I am calling in help from two New Testament texts, Matthew 5:27–30, Jesus' interpretation of the commandment in His Sermon on the Mount; and 1 Corinthians 6:12–20, the Apostle Paul's theology of the human body.

Whenever we wrestle with any of God's commandments (be they in the Old or New Testaments), we need to keep in mind two things about the commandment.

First, we need to keep in mind God's motivation in giving the commands. It is love and love's desire for our freedom. The Lawgiver loves us and does not want us to ruin our lives. Yahweh

---

1 In that sermon series I heard him give in 1972.

loves us and wants us to enjoy to the fullest the life for which we were created and are being redeemed. God really wants us to live fully human lives.

Therefore, when we read, "You shall not commit adultery," we are not to think, as many people think, that God is against sex. Many people react to the seventh commandment as though the Living God were the cosmic killjoy, out to squelch whatever fun we creatures find in this broken world. But God is not against sex. Quite the contrary! Just read the Song of Solomon some time! I would not be able to read the text out loud to you without blushing. In the Song of Solomon we find God rejoicing in the passionate and tender lovemaking of husband and wife. Or read in the book of Proverbs sayings like these:

> Let your fountain be blessed,
> And rejoice in the wife of your youth.
> As a loving hind and a graceful doe,
> Let her breasts satisfy you at all times;
> Be exhilarated always with her love.

> Proverbs 5:18–19

Yes! Those words are in the Bible! God is not out to ruin sex. After all, God created men and women for each other (Genesis 2:18–23). Yahweh the Lawgiver is the One who made us sexual beings, and He is the one who said, "Behold, it was very good" (Genesis 1:31).

Again, when Yahweh commands, "You shall not commit adultery," Yahweh does so for our good to protect and enhance our sexuality. As though the Manufacturer were saying, "Powerful gift. Handle with care!"

The second thing we need to keep in mind about God's commandments is that they emerge from God's character. God did not one day dream up a bunch of rules and then impose them on us. Yahweh's commandments flow from Yahweh's character; they spill over from who God is. The seventh commandment flows *out of God's faithfulness.* Yahweh is the God who keeps promises, the God who makes and keeps covenants, the God who does not turn away from or cheat against His beloved.

The seventh commandment also flows *out of God's jealousy.* "I, Yahweh your God, am a jealous God" (Exodus 20:5). God's jealousy is God's zeal to protect what is supremely precious.[2] Yahweh loves us so much that He will not tolerate rival gods, rival loves, coming between Him and His beloved.

And the seventh commandment flows *from God's oneness:* "Hear, O Israel, Yahweh your God is one" (Deuteronomy 6:4). "Let us make humanity in our image" (Genesis 1:26). Yahweh is the one God who exists in fellowship, in community, as the Triune God: Father, Son, and Holy Spirit. Yahweh is the God of committed love, of total oneness of heart and mind.[3]

As creatures created in this God's image, and as people redeemed by this God's mercy, we are to reflect in our relationships God's faithfulness, passionate jealousy, and oneness. We are commanded to not commit adultery because Yahweh would never do so to us.

Let us now grapple with the seventh commandment head on. Let us do so by asking two questions: First, What is the Creator's

---

2 J.I. Packer, op.cit.

3 See my *Experiencing the Trinity,* Canadian Church Leaders Network; 2nd ed. edition (2021).

intention in this commandment? That is, what is Yahweh after here?

Second, How can we live out that intention in our sexually super-charged era? How can we obey this "culture of adultery"?

1. What is the Creator's intention? What is God after?

We get at the answer by first understanding how the commandment was understood by those who first received it. And then when we hear what Jesus, the Lawgiver in human flesh, does with it in His Sermon on the Mount.

Consider first the historical/sociological context. Women of that time were considered to be the property of a man. A woman was her father's property until she married, when she then became the property of her husband. (Property: That's what she was. And she could be sold without her consent.)

Therefore, adultery with another man's wife simply constituted a violation of that man's property rights. The males who first heard the commandment took it to prohibit the infringement of another man's rights; there was no thought of the women's rights (she had none). That is, males understood the seventh commandment in a very narrow sense: sexual intercourse with the wife of another man was prohibited because it violated property rights. So, for instance, males did not take the commandment as prohibiting sex with a prostitute. A man could have a fling on the town with a clear conscience, for he had not violated anyone's property rights.

Males did, however, understand the seventh commandment as binding the woman to unconditional fidelity. She was his and his alone. But he was not hers and hers alone.

So the Lawgiver comes down from the mountain top. He comes all the way down. He comes into our flesh and blood as Jesus of Nazareth. And in His Sermon on the Mount He helps males see that they had grossly mistaken the intent of the seventh commandment.

> "You have heard that it was said, 'You shall not commit adultery'; but I say to you,....." [Here Jesus is claiming the right to give an authoritative interpretation of the Law.] "...that every one who looks on a woman to lust for her has committed adultery with her already in his heart."
>
> Matthew 5:27–28

Jesus corrects the mistaken understanding of the Law in two ways, and thereby intensifies the commandment in two ways:

Jesus challenges the supposed right of a male to sexual freedom outside marriage. As one scholar puts it, "Like the wife, the husband is under an obligation of fidelity. The wife is exalted to the same dignity as the husband."[4] Jesus delivers the woman from the status of a thing to fulfill the desires of men, to a real person, with her own rights. Extramarital and unnatural intercourse constitutes not a violation of another man's property rights; it is, rather, a violation of a commitment to a person, a violation of the woman's right to exclusive sexual union.

And Jesus intensifies the seventh commandment by deepening the meaning of adultery. "Adultery does not consist merely in physical intercourse with a strange woman; it is present

---

4 Friedrich Hauck, "pornea", *Theological Dictionary of the New Testament*. *Vol. VI* (Grand Rapids: Eerdmans, 1968), 733.

already in the desire which negates fidelity."[5] Genital penetration is not the line that separates faithfulness and unfaithfulness. The line is crossed whenever a man lusts for another woman. Joy Davidman argued that Jesus has defined adultery "...as a certain view of women, rather than as a certain act."[6]

Remember: the Living God speaks the seventh commandment, and its intensification, out of love. The Creator, who is our Redeemer, really wants the best for us. So E. Stanley Jones can say that Jesus "is not being ascetic but aseptic."[7] Jesus is not speaking as a reclusive monk but as a doctor seeking our health.

I need to be careful here or I, too, might get crucified with Jimmy Carter. What does Jesus mean by "lust"? He means desire, but a particular kind of desire: the desire to possess, the desire to take for oneself, the desire to use the other for one's own self-gratification. Appreciation for another person is one thing; lust is another all together. Lust is self-centered and self-seeking desire. Lust wants the other person in order to fulfill one's own needs.

It is helpful to translate Jesus' words literally. "Whoever keeps on looking at a woman *in order* to lust after her." Jesus is not speaking about the appreciative glance at a beautiful person. Rather, Jesus is speaking about the willful, sustained stare, the look which goes beyond appreciative to the desire to possess. "Looking at a beautiful person is a drive given in creation; staring

---

5 Ibid, 734.

6 Joy Davidman, *Smoke on the Mountain: An Interpretation of the Ten Commandments* (Philadelphia: Westminster Press, 1954), 88.

7 E. Stanley Jones, *Christ of the Mount: A Working Philosophy of Life* (New York, Cincinnati [etc.]: The Abingdon Press, 1931), 146.

or leering is a drive given in the fall from creation."[8]

Why is lust such a problem? Why does Jesus come down so hard on it? For a married person, lustful desire for another person pulls one away from unconditional commitment to one's spouse. Desiring another man or woman drives a wedge between spouses, which, during the time of desiring, borders on the damage caused by an outright affair. The act of adultery is not needed to adulterate marriage. Thinking lustfully about the other man or woman automatically robs one's spouse of the emotional attention and affection he or she rightly deserves.

Furthermore, lust is problematic because it uses the other person's sexuality as a means to the end of one's own self-gratification. It reduces the other person to less than a person—to a mere object. That is the inhumanity of pornography: persons reduced to objects.

In equating lust and adultery, Jesus is driving home the original intent of the seventh commandment: unconditional faithfulness to the person of the other. We were made in such a way that our sexuality is protected, and thereby nurtured, in the exclusivity of the one-man, one-woman covenant of marriage. Sexual intercourse outside of or before marriage breaks that exclusivity; so does lusting for another woman or man.

So we can restate the seventh commandment positively: "Your sexuality thrives in the context of unconditional commitment."

---

8 F. Dale Bruner, op. cit., 183.

2. How then can we live out the Creator's intention in our sexually supercharged era?

As C. S. Lewis so aptly observed, "We grow up surrounded by propaganda in favor of unchastity."[9] And Lewis wrote that in the late 1950's, long before the rise of online pornography, smart phones, and social media apps designed to addict and seduce people. From nearly every corner of our world we are bombarded with messages encouraging us to go against the good Law of the good Creator.

So how do we live in obedience in such an environment?

Let me suggest six things we can do. The sixth is most crucial.

(A) First, identify the pressures on us. Call a spade a spade and tell it like it is. Often just naming the enemy can give us a measure of victory over it. Dr. Lewis Smedes (then Professor of Ethics at Fuller Theological Seminary) wrote a helpful book entitled, "*Sex for Christians.*" In it he names many of the pressures. He is careful to remind us that "pressures are not excuses. They are only factors in people's lives that sometimes shove them toward adultery...they do make people vulnerable."[10]

Smedes divides the pressures into two kinds—external and internal.

He first identifies some of the external forces. They include the sexualized atmosphere: our society puts a premium on sexual fulfillment. Sexual convenience: in Smedes' words, "We are mobile: we can get away easily to places where we will not be

---

9 C. S. Lewis, *Mere Christianity* (New York: MacMillan Company, 1953), 74.
10 Lewis B. Smedes, *Sex for Christians: The Limits and Liberties of Sexual Living* (Grand Rapids: Eerdmans, First edition, 1976), 196. (I recommend the first edition.)

seen. We are affluent: we can pay for the secret lunches and hotel rooms. We are free from worry about pregnancy; we have the pill.". Sexual contact: we have more opportunities to be with sexually interesting people. The list goes on. Community erosion: neighbors no longer care about our moral behavior; the church has lost its moral clout in the community. And the biggest pressure: we are sold the bill of goods that marriage is only fulfilling if shot through with erotic ecstasy. So when the romance wears off, we have, says Smedes, the "constitutional right" to recover it.

Then Smedes names internal pressures. They include: anger, self-hatred, perfectionism, escapism, sexual deviations, boredom, sexual deprivation (spouse withholding sex), emotional deprivation (the longing for genuine communication and sharing of feelings), self-doubt, unequal growth (one spouse growing intellectually while the other stagnates), creeping old age, and an independent spirit. None of these justifies disobedience. But they do put pressure on us to buy into the propaganda.

(B) Secondly, we can expose the current "myths" about human sexuality. Example: "Sexual activity quiets inner turmoil." For many people, copulation has become a pacifier. How many movies or television programs drive this home? Another example: "If you're not sexually fulfilled, you're not fully human." If you do not have sex two or three times a week, you are missing out on life. Although we are sexual beings, the actual act of intercourse does not bring us to human fullness. We need only look at Jesus, or Paul, or Mother Teresa to dispel that myth. Another: "I can't do anything about my feelings. They are there and must be expressed." Such a statement reveals profound slavery—slavery to feelings, to drives, to desires. Freedom is the ability to transcend compulsion. What is going to control my life?

My biological drives, or what I know to be right before God? My feelings or my will?

Here are some more. "I love my wife and children and do not want a divorce, so it is better that I have an affair for the sake of my family." "My husband is not fulfilling me sexually, so it is okay to find sexual satisfaction instead of divorcing my husband."[11]

Here is the biggest myth of all: "Sexual intercourse is just a passing biological contact." It is a very old myth. It was circulating at the church in the first-century city of Corinth. The Apostle Paul explodes that myth when he writes: "The body is not for immorality, but for the Lord; and the Lord is for the body.... Do you not know that your bodies are members of Christ? Shall I then take away the members of Christ and make them members of a harlot? May it never be! Or do you not know that the one who joins himself to a harlot is one body with her? For God says, 'The two shall become one flesh.' ...Every other sin that a person commits is outside the body, but the immoral person sins against his own body" (1 Corinthians 6:13–18).

Paul is saying that something happens in intercourse between a man and a woman that is more than biology. Which is why two people do not feel the same way about each other afterward. There is a mysterious, invisible sharing of one's very self, not just the sharing of parts of the flesh. Paul says that sexual sin is a sin "against one's own body." The word he uses is *sōma*, from which we get the English word "somatic." It refers to the whole person, to the whole personality, to the person as a person

---

11 Laura Schlessinger, *The Ten Commandments: The Significance of God's Laws In Everyday Life* (Thorndike, Maine: Thorndike Press, 1999), 227.

meant for God.[12] For Paul, I do not *have* a *sōma*, a body; I *am* a *sōma*, a body. What I do with my body, I do with me. Paul is not saying that adultery is the worst sin. He is saying that adultery strikes more deeply at the root of our personhood than any other sin. A part of one's very self is given away in sexual intercourse. And it cannot be taken back.

Because of this mysterious sharing of "selves" in sexual intercourse, the Creator, who loves us and wants our best, sets up a protective shield: "You shall not commit adultery." "I do not want to see you destroy your *sōma*—your very self."

There is more to sex than biology. That warning needs to be sounded again and again. Our society is buying into a horrible myth that destroys God's beautiful creation.

> He who commits adultery has no sense;
> He who does it destroys himself.
>
> Proverbs 6:32

Identify the pressures. Expose and defuse the myths.

(C) Third, as a friend of mine says, "Acts do not come out of nowhere." The act of adultery does not come out of nowhere. The act of adultery comes out of adultery in the heart.

Dr. Paul Mickey, then of Duke University, shares in his book, *Tough Marriage*, the observation, "In my counseling experience, an extramarital sex act is rarely the first expression of lust in a person's life. It is usually the last."

---

12 Leon Morris, *The First Epistle of Paul to the Corinthians; An Introduction and Commentary*, The Tyndale New Testament Commentaries Series (Grand Rapids: Eerdmans, 1958), 100.

Dr. Mickey speaks of what he calls "the domino effect":

Domino #1: You begin to fantasize about some sort of illicit, extramarital sex. This could happen after you take in information of stimulation—such as through movies, television, soft-core magazines, or some other outside source. Or you might just take a 'mental trip' back to an old love affair or to some other sexually stimulating event.

Domino #2: You become preoccupied for periods of time with lust and fantasy so that you begin to engage in self-gratification. This can be going on even when having relations with one's spouse—it's just that fantasy, and not love, is the driving force.

Domino #3: Your sexual fantasy life and periods of self-gratification increase in scope, mainly because you are becoming desensitized. The initial pleasure you got from your fantasies just isn't enough anymore.

Domino #4: You begin to look around for more sexual excitement outside the home. It may be more voyeurism than direct involvement at first—such as going to porno movies or live sex shows.

Domino #5: Finally, looking just can't satisfy you anymore, so you decide the time has come to take a little action. ...Often only half-consciously, you begin to look for opportunities; and sure enough, they begin to come your way.[13]

Whatever happens at that point we have taken the decisive step from fantasy to action.

---

13 Paul Mickey, *Tough Marriage: How to Make a Difficult Relationship Work* (New York: Bantam Publishers, 1987).

Jesus therefore exhorts us, "stop the process at the first domino." Stop the process at the point of fantasy. Martin Luther, commenting on Jesus' words, quotes an early church historian who said, "I cannot keep a bird from flying over my head. But I can certainly keep it from nesting in my hair or from biting my nose off."

Acts do not come from nowhere. The issue is always our hearts.

(D) Which brings us to the fourth thing we can do to live out God's good intention. We can welcome, and cooperate with, the grace and power of the Holy Spirit. In his letter to the believers in Corinth, which I quoted earlier, Paul asks: "Do you not know that your body is a temple of the Holy Spirit who is in you...?" (1 Corinthians 6:19). It is one of the most powerful questions we can ever ask. When you and I respond to Jesus Christ and give Him our lives, He gives us His life in the Person of the Holy Spirit. The Spirit then takes up residence within us, in our hearts, in our *sōmas*. Do you not know that your body is the dwelling place of the third Person of the Holy Trinity?

As we open ourselves up to the Spirit's Presence and Power, He begins to work with our desires; He begins to bring our drives back into line with His will. The result is what Paul calls the "fruit of the Spirit." The very qualities we need in order to obey God's commands: "love, patience, faithfulness, self-control" (Galatians 5:22–23). The Spirit can keep our longings and drives in check. The Spirit can channel our longings and desires to flow with God's will. The Spirit can give us strength to be faithful. Jesus breathes into our bodies the power of the Creator to obey the Creator of our sexuality. Sin has twisted our sexual instinct; the Spirit can untwist it and make it whole again.

(E) The fifth thing we can do: we can make it a whole lot "easier" for the Holy Spirit by staying away from the places, pictures, or people that arouse wrong desire. If certain television programs stimulate lust, turn them off. That is what Jesus means when He commands us to "tear it [your eye] out and throw it from you" (Matthew 5:29). If certain films arouse passion, do not go. To paraphrase Jesus, "It is better to miss out on the latest best picture than to wrestle with distorted sexuality." If the Internet is causing you to stumble, either get someone to put a block on it against pornography, or we get rid of it altogether. I think that is what Jesus means by "cut off your right hand" (Matthew 5:30). "Flee immorality," says Paul. Turn your back on it and walk away. Turn around and run to Jesus, the passionately jealous lover of our souls.

Identify the pressures. Expose the myths. Remember that acts do not come out of nowhere. Open up to the Spirit of God. Stay away from the things that quicken lust.

(F) And sixth, and most crucial, realize why the Creator made us sexual beings. I am thinking of two things here. First, our sexuality reflects something of the Being of God. God has made us in God's image. "So God created humankind in His image, in the image of God He created them; male and female he created them" (Genesis 1:27). Something about the two sexes sharing life in tenderness and total-life commitment reflects the fellowship within the Triune God.

But secondly, there is an even deeper intention for our sexuality. Sexual desire is a symptom of our desire for God. It is significant to note that the Hebrew word for "knowing" in "knowing God," is the same word used to describe the sexual intimacy between husband and wife. "Now the man knew his wife Eve, and she conceived..." (Genesis 4:1).

Sexual joy is given to us by God to prepare us for the joy of knowing God, compared to which, "the most rapturous love between a man and a woman on this earth is mere milk and water."[14] Sexual longing is a symptom of, and points toward, the deeper longing to know God in intimacy and trust.

Have you ever thought of sexual desire in that way? What Yahweh our Creator wants for us, more than anything else, is the joy of intimacy with Him. That is why "You shall not commit adultery" is not the first commandment. The first commandment is "You shall have no other gods before Me." Yahweh is the passionately jealous lover of our souls who constantly beckons us to come and enjoy His love. If I am having trouble with sexual desires, if they are aflame and out of control, it is but a sign that my spirit is hungering for God, and that it has been a long time since I really enjoyed God. The thing to do then is not to seek some biological outlet. The thing to do is seek the love of the Living God. Sexual passion is a symptom of the deeper passion for God.

You can see then why fast-moving high achievers are especially vulnerable to inappropriate sexual fantasy and activity. We have been driving so hard for so long that we have slowly but surely created a vacuum in the soul—a vacuum into which lust and all its false promises easily enter. And you can see why spouses and children of high achievers are so vulnerable; they have not been pursued or cared for in a long time.[15]

---

14 C. S. Lewis, *Mere Christianity* (New York: MacMillan Company, 1953), 84. For a fuller expansion of this idea, see James A. K. Smith, *You Are What You Love* (Brazos, 2016).

15 I owe this insight to George Barna.

Desire for sexual intimacy is a symptom of the desire for intimacy with God.

Which is why God does not call us to stuff or stifle sexual desire. Instead, God calls us to recognize what is going on in our hearts. We are longing for God. G. K. Chesterton could say, "Everyone who knocks at the door of a brothel is looking for God."

Jesus Christ, the Lawgiver who comes to us in our flesh and blood, and with all seriousness calls us to the mystery of human sexuality. And when we mess it up, with equal seriousness, He offers forgiveness and cleansing. To the village prostitute, "Woman, your sins have been forgiven." (Luke 7:48). To the woman whom Pharisees had caught in the act of adultery and brought to Jesus, He says, "Neither do I condemn you" (John 8:11). For the repentant there is forgiveness and cleansing. There is healing and a fresh start.

And there is the reaffirmation of the goodness of the seventh commandment. For Jesus goes on to say to the woman, and what he would have said to the man if the man had stuck around, "Go your way. From now on sin no more" (John 8:11).

EXODUS 20:15

"You shall not steal."

KLEPTOMANIA:
THE DISEASE OF UN-FAITH

In his letter to the Galatians, in what many call "The Magna Carta of Christian Liberty," the Apostle Paul makes an amazing claim about the Ten Commandments. In Galatians 3:24, Paul refers to the Law as, "Our tutor to lead us to Christ."

I don't know about you, but the Law is serving me as just such a tutor in a big way. This series of studies in the Ten Commandments has awakened in me a fresh, deep, ravenous hunger for Jesus Christ and His grace. Seriously studying the Law has shown me just how far short I fall from the Creator's design for human life as we have it articulated in the commandments. AND studying the Law has once again revealed just how impotent I am to live up to that design on my own; I simply cannot meet the Law's good demands on my own; I need help from outside myself.

The Law is exercising its tutorial function in me by kindling a fresh longing for a Savior. I long for Someone who forgives me for falling short, and who accepts me in my failure, and who can then empower me to live the good life of the good Law.

This series of studies in the Ten Commandments has driven me to the Apostle Paul's letter to the Romans. In Romans, Paul wrestles with his, and my, failure and impotence before the Law. And in Romans he declares incredibly good news:

> Therefore there is now no condemnation at all for those who are in Christ Jesus. For the law of the Spirit of life in Christ Jesus has set you free from the law of sin and of death. For what the law could not do, weak as it was through the flesh, God did: sending His own Son in the likeness of sinful flesh and as an offering for sin, He condemned sin in the flesh, in order that the requirement of the Law might be fulfilled in us, who do not walk according to the flesh [who do not rely on their own resources], but [who walk] according to the Spirit [who rely on the resources of the Spirit].
>
> Romans 8:1–4

Ah...wonderful news! In Jesus Christ, the Lawgiver forgives our failure and empowers us to live the Law. In Jesus Christ, the Lawgiver gives us the Holy Spirit, first of all as the seal of our forgiveness, and then as the Divine resource to live a fully human life.

Long ago the prophet Ezekiel recorded God's promise to one day create a new heart in His people, and to put a new spirit, God's Spirit, within that new heart. As a result of that gracious work, God said, "...I will cause you to walk in my statutes..." (Ezekiel 36:27). In Jesus Christ that great promise is being fulfilled!

Let us turn to the tutor again, to the tutor who always leads us to Christ. In this chapter let us submit ourselves to the tutorial work of the eighth commandment, "You shall not steal."

At first glance the eighth commandment does not appear to be all that challenging or relevant. In fact, I considered dealing with this commandment in connection with the chapter on the tenth commandment, "You shall not covet." I mean, what possible relevance does this commandment have for decent, hard-working, law-abiding citizens like you and me? Oh, many of us have been on the "receiving" end of the disobedience of the commandment. Many of us have been victims of stealing. When Sharon and I were living in West Los Angeles, we came home from Thanksgiving dinner at her parents' home to find our home burglarized. On the first day we had moved to Glendale, our son David's mountain bike was stolen off the front lawn. When we returned from a recent trip our garage in Vancouver had been broken into, and all my tools were gone. So, many of us can identify with the result of disobedience of the eighth commandment. But can we identify with the other end, the "giving" end of stealing? We are not bank robbers, or home burglars, or shoplifters...are we? How does the eighth commandment speak to us?

As I have worked on the commandment, (or, as I should say, as the commandment has worked on me) I have become impressed by how wide the scope of the commandment is. It turns out that the eighth commandment speaks a very relevant, very challenging word to decent, law-abiding people.

The challenge comes to us in two ways:

First, by understanding the in-depth meaning of the actual word used in the commandment.

Second, by recognizing the issues which undergird and/or spin out from the commandment.

Let us first try to understand the in-depth meaning of the word translated "steal."

Old Testament scholar Brevard Childs notes that the Hebrew word used in the law (*ganab*) has a particular nuance of meaning that distinguishes it from other Hebrew words we translate as "steal."[1] That distinguishing nuance is the element of secrecy. The verb refers not only to the violent act of snatching another person's property, but refers to the subtle, secretive taking of what is not one's own.

This nuance is more clearly seen in the Greek word used to translate the Hebrew word. It is the verb *klepto*, from which we get our English words kleptomaniac and kleptomania. *Klepto* means to steal "secretly and craftily."[2] *Klepto* also has the following other meanings: to deceive, cheat, bewitch (by flattery); to hold secretly, to put away, to conceal, to hide; to do something in a shifty manner.

With that range of meanings, all of a sudden the eighth commandment starts to get close to home; the law has gone from preaching to meddling! For what Yahweh our Creator prohibits here is not only the overt, violent seizing of another's property; Yahweh prohibits the deeper, hidden, subtle, crafty taking or keeping of what is not our own. In that light then, kleptomania is much more than shoplifting, or bank robbery, or home burglary; it is the secret desire to take, to possess, to hold, or to keep. It is very close to coveting, the concern of the tenth commandment.

Jesus brings out this in-depth meaning of the word "steal"

---

1 Brevard S. Childs, *The Book of Exodus: A Critical, Theological Commentary* (Philadelphia: Westminster Press, 1974), 423.
2 Carl Heinz Peisker, "klepto", *Theological Dictionary of the New Testament, Volume III* (Grand Rapids: Eerdmans, 1964), 754.

when He drives the money changers out of the Temple calling them "thieves" (Mark 11:17), "stealers." Why were they thieves? What were they doing? They were only selling animals for the religious sacrifices, but at hugely-inflated prices. They were only exchanging foreign currency for the correct temple currency, but they were charging an unreasonable fee for the service. Such acts, such "normal" business acts, Jesus labels "stealing." Shrewd financiers, tolerated by the religious community, Jesus calls kleptomaniacs.

Think with me for a moment about some of the crafty acts that we tolerate in our day. What does Jesus call such acts?

What about using phones and social media excessively during work time? Is that not stealing? What about employees, who have contracted to do so many hours of work for so much pay, that are leaving early, extending breaks, or allowing personal tasks to invade times that they work from home? Is that not stealing? What about illegal streaming, downloading, and all the other opportunities the internet has appointed us? Are those not robbing the creators of their fair pay? Such crafty ways to get something for nothing! What about parking in handicapped spots when we are not legally in need?

What about plagiarism, using another person's work without acknowledging it? It happens in the church more than we care to know. Bruce Thielman, one of the most powerful orators of the twentieth century, was visiting a church in the Midwest one Sunday morning. The preacher got up and opened the sermon with an illustration Bruce had used to open his sermon on the same text. The preacher then developed the first point in the sermon the same way Bruce had in his sermon. The preacher developed the second point just the way Bruce had in his sermon. On it went to having the identical conclusion. The man had preached Bruce's sermon without even mentioning Bruce's name! After the service Bruce went up to the preacher and said, "Hi! I am Bruce Thielman. The Lord has mercy on you."

What about stretching loopholes in the tax laws? Maybe it can be argued that the stretching is legal, but is it not a crafty way to take, or keep, what is not our own? What about accepting benefit or welfare checks when one is no longer legally eligible? What about abusing lenient return policies for stores and products? Someone will have to make up for that loss at the end of the day. What about selling a used car without telling the whole story about the car's problems? Is that not robbing the buyer of the difference between what he or she paid and what he or she should have paid had the cost been set with all the facts known? Subtle, this kleptomania, isn't it?

What about fudging on contracts, inflating prices, skimping on quality of the parts? What about selling people things they really do not need? There are a lot of thieves on Madison Avenue are there not? Religious businesses stand under the same judgment. What about selling poor folks in the south one-hundred-dollar gold-leaf Bibles, which most cannot read anyway? Crafty!

What about soliciting funds, even for missions, by subtle guilt pressure? What about gossip? Does not gossip rob a person's character? Does not gossip "steal a reputation?" asks J. I. Packer.[3]

We could go on and on. See how much of life the eighth commandment touches?

---

3 I heard him say this in a lecture.

The ultimate forms of theft are, of course, kidnapping and slavery. For them a person is robbed of his or her right to his or her body.

"You shall not steal." It is an unconditional command. No amount of subtle rationalization changes it. For the commandment addresses the very subtlety we use to justify taking what is not our own.

The heat is turned up when we recognize the original context into which Yahweh spoke this commandment. According to Old Testament scholar Ronald Wallace, the background for "You shall not steal," "was one in which there always tended to appear extreme differences in wealth and poverty."[4] Those "who had position, ability and resources, instead of using them for the good of their neighbors, were tempted to use them to draw into their own power and possession what their brother (or sister) possessed too."[5] "As the wealth of the country developed through trade and commerce, instead of benefiting all members of the community, it tended to flow into the hands of those at the top of the social scale, where it largely remained."[6]

The commandment addresses *that* context—the rich getting richer while the poor are getting poorer. Actually, the context was worse than that. It was the *redeemed rich* who were getting richer while the *redeemed poor* were getting poorer. So, Ronald Wallace paraphrases Yahweh's concern this way: "I have not redeemed your brother that he might lie starving and exposed under your feet. Nor have I been especially generous to you, in order to put

---

4 Ronald S. Wallace, *The Ten Commandments: A Study of Ethical Freedom* (Grand Rapids: Eerdmans, 1965), 152.
5 Ibid.
6 Ibid, 153.

power in your hands further to inflict him. Give to your brother what he needs for his welfare out of what you have, for what you have is mine, and to withhold your hand from him is to steal from Me!"[7]

As I have been trying to show throughout this book, the commandments emerge from the Lawgiver's character: "You shall not commit adultery." Why? Because Yahweh never would commit adultery. "You shall not steal." Why? Because Yahweh never would steal. God never takes what is not His own. And He calls His people to reflect the same character in their relationships with others. Jesus calls Himself "the Good Shepherd," who—in contrast to the false shepherd who comes to steal and destroy—comes to give, to lay down His life for the sheep: "I came that they might have life and have it abundantly" (John 10:10–11).

The challenge of the eighth commandment also comes to us by recognizing the issues which undergird and spin out from it. I want to identify five. There are many more; the more you reflect on the commandment the more you discover!

(1) First, the eighth commandment affirms private property. Here our Creator and Lord affirms our creatureliness: we are beings who need shelter, clothing, food, and land. Here Yahweh affirms that it is right to desire creature comforts.

Another way of expressing this first issue is to say, there is nothing inherently wrong with having possessions. In some Christian circles, people are made to feel guilty if they have anything nice. Such Christians often point to the book of Acts, where the first Christians sold all of their possessions—their homes and land—and then shared them in common. So, it is

---

7 Ibid, 156.

argued, Jesus Christ calls us to renounce all privately-held property. But what such an argument fails to observe is (1) that selling of their property was totally voluntary; it was not a requirement of discipleship. And (2) it fails to observe that the early church held worship services in individual member's homes; meaning that some did not sell their houses. They may have kept their homes but did not treat their homes as private castles, but as ministry centers, "half-way" houses for men and women whom Jesus was redeeming.

The eighth commandment is rightly taken by many economists as an affirmation of the legitimacy of private property.

However, we must carefully note that the eighth commandment does not declare the absolute right to private property. This commandment does not affirm the absolute sanctity of private ownership of land or possessions. That idea is the child of Adam Smith, the eighteenth-century philosopher/economist, not the child of Jesus Christ. For we must remember that in the Hebrew view of reality, Yahweh—the Living God—is alone the absolute owner. "The earth is Yahweh's, and all it contains; the world, and those who dwell in it" (Psalm 24:1). Yahweh alone has an absolute right to property. And, "...this Absolute Owner places *significant limitations* on how his people acquire and use *His* property."[8] This means that it is theologically incorrect for any human to ever use the word "own" of anything! For theologically *all we have and are is God's and has been entrusted to us.*

To make sure that Israel, and by extension the new Israel, the Church, understood this, Yahweh established two institutions:

---

8 Ronald Sider, *Rich Christians in an Age of Hunger: A Biblical Study* (Downers Grove, Illinois: Inter-Varsity Press, 1984), 115; emphasis mine.

the sabbatical year and the year of Jubilee. Every seven years the land was to lay fallow. Why? God says: "So that the needy of your people may eat" (Exodus 23:11). Every seventh year the poor were given free run of whatever naturally grew on the fields. And every seven years *all debts* were canceled (see Deuteronomy 15:1–6)! Yahweh even made it clear that you could not refuse to give a poor man a loan the sixth year knowing that it would be canceled the seventh.[9]

Then, every fifty years Israel was to hold the Jubilee. In the Jubilee year all land was to be returned to the original owners (Leviticus 25). Why? To remind Israel that land cannot be sold permanently because Yahweh is the One who owns it (Leviticus 25:23). These two institutions kept the people mindful of who the real Owner was; and these two institutions kept the gap between rich and poor from widening too far.

We can summarize the first issue involved in the eighth commandment in the words of Joy Davidman: "Property is neither sin nor inalienable right, but a loan, a trust from God."[10]

(2) Second, the eighth commandment reminds us that we are stewards of the earth. "Stewardship" is not just a once-a-year concept. "Stewardship" is to be a lifestyle, a worldview. We are called by the Creator and Lord of the earth to see all that we have and are as gifts from God; gifts to be employed for God's purposes. We are accountable to the Owner for our stewardship: how did I use what was entrusted to me? Jesus taught the Parable of the Talents to make that point (Matthew 25:14ff). The one who hears Jesus', "Well done, good and faithful steward," is the

9 Ibid, 90-92.
10 Davidman, op.cit., 99.

one who uses his money (a talent was one thousand dollars in silver) for the Master, to increase the Master's wealth. "One day I shall be asked to give an account of how I managed those of His resources of which I was given control."[11]

We are stewards, not owners. The fact is, it is very possible for a steward to steal the Master's property, either overtly or subtly. God asks Israel through the prophet Malachi: "Will a human being rob God?" What a ridiculous question! How in the world can humans rob God? Yet, God asks it, and goes on to answer the question Himself: "Yet you are robbing Me! Startled, Israel asks, "How have we robbed You?" God's answer: "In tithes and offerings" (Malachi 3:8). Israel was stealing from God by not returning to Him the tithe—the first ten percent. God owns it all; but the first ten percent is especially God's. Giving the tithe was a sign that Israel recognized Yahweh's absolute ownership. The real question to ask then is not, "How much should I give to God" but "How much would God want me to keep for myself?" It is all Yahweh's; we are but stewards.

(3) Third, the eighth commandment reminds us that we live interconnected lives. What we do with our property (or I should say God's property entrusted to our stewardship) affects other people. We live in a "global village;" we need to evaluate our stewardship of property in light of that fact.

What does this mean? Well, as we said earlier, there is nothing inherently wrong with having many possessions. In fact, it can at times be a sign of God's blessing upon us. But, when the majority of the people of the world are hungry and cold, having many possessions takes on a different value. I really like our

---

11 Again, I heard J. I. Packer share this in a lecture.

comfortable affluence in North America. I really desire such a life. Now, if I just see my lifestyle in the light of North America I have no trouble with it. And I believe that if the whole world were like North America, God would not have trouble with it either (except for the fact that He is ignored in most of it!). But we must face the fact that the rest of the world is not like the comfortable cities of North America at all. To continue to sustain our way of life without a concern for the rest of the world is kleptomania—stealing. Martin Luther once said: "If our goods are not available to the community, then they are stolen goods."[12]

God blesses people so that they/we become blessings. To not let the blessing become a blessing is to steal the blessing. "Though water left to itself always tends to flow downwards, money, on the contrary, always tends to flow upwards to those who have it."[13] Kleptomania involves craftily holding-on-to as well as taking-away-from. We live an interconnected life.

(4) Fourth, the eighth commandment warns us against our greed. The eighth commandment warns us of the seductive power of property. The same power which seduces the thief to steal can seduce us to cling /too tightly/ to what God has entrusted to us. Moses gave the following warning to Israel as they were about to enter the Promised Land:

> "Beware lest you forget Yahweh...lest, when you have eaten and are satisfied, and have built good houses and lived in them, and when your herds and your flocks multiply, and your silver and

---

12 Quoted by Richard Foster in *Celebration of Discipline: The Path to Spiritual Growth* (San Francisco: Harper & Row, 1988), 78.
13 Wallace, op. cit., 155.

gold multiply, and all that you have multiplies, then your heart becomes proud, and you forget Yahweh your God.... Otherwise, you may say in your heart 'My power and the strength of my hand made me this wealth.' But you shall remember Yahweh your God, for it is He who is giving you power to make wealth...."

Deuteronomy 8:11–17

How contemporary! Israel was warned against beginning to think that her wealth was the ground of her security. Israel was warned against beginning to think that she was a "self-made nation."

Again, let me say, there is nothing inherently evil about possessions. Nevertheless, possessions have a seductive power— the power to move us toward idolizing possessions, and thus thinking we do not need the Living God. (See Colossians 3:5; Ephesians 5:5.) Thus Paul told Timothy, a young pastor in the Ephesian church: "Instruct those who are rich in this present world not to be conceited or fix their hope on the uncertainty of riches, but on God, who richly supplies us with all things to enjoy" (1 Timothy 6:17).

It is interesting to observe that percentage-wise Jesus had more to say about money and property than anything else. Why? Because our feelings about our possessions and the possessions of others is a very accurate indicator of our spiritual vitality. St. Augustine calls our possessions the rings of love from Yahweh our Beloved. But they are only rings; they are not the Beloved Himself.[14]

---

14 Quoted by Ronald Sider, op. cit., 125.

(5) Fifth, the eighth commandment calls us to put our trust in Yahweh the Provider. The commandment is addressing that deep sense of insecurity we have, that basic anxiety about the future. "The Lord, Yahweh, is my shepherd," says the Psalmist. And because Yahweh is, "I shall not want—I will have all I need." Paul tells the Philippians: "...My God shall supply all your needs according to His riches in glory in Christ Jesus" (Philippians 4:19). In Jesus Christ, God is committed to taking care of His people. Therefore, we need not overtly or secretly take away from others or keep only for ourselves.

Whenever I steal (or tightly hold) it says I have concluded three things:

(A) First, I have concluded that God is not all that good; Yahweh is not really committed to my welfare.

(B) Second, I have concluded that the Living God cannot be trusted. It is not that God is too slow in meeting my needs; it is that God simply cannot be trusted.

(C) So third, I must then take matters into my own hands. I must grab for and keep all of the gusto I can, for only I can be trusted to take care of my family and myself.

What a terrifying state of mind it is that moves us to steal; what fear, the fear of being left out, or left without. What an equally-terrifying state of mind it is that moves a person to clutch his or her possessions tightly. In 1980, I heard James Houston, then the President of Regent College in Vancouver, British Columbia, say, "all possessiveness is born of fear." He has proved to be right. I only cling to what I think I own in the face of other people's needs, because I fear the consequences for my family and myself if I were to give it away. I only take what is not my own because I fear that I will miss out on life without those things.

Kleptomania, therefore, is the disease of un-faith.

So the writer of the book of Hebrews exhorts us: "Let your character be free from the love of money, being content with what you have." We ask "How?" Oh dear God, how can I be free to be content? The writer answers: "For God Himself has said, 'I will never desert you, nor will I forsake you,' so that we can confidently say, 'The Lord is my helper, I will not fear'" (Hebrews 13:5–6).

Bottom line: can I trust the God who comes to me in Jesus Christ to take care of me and my family, or do I need to steal, either by taking or keeping?

The Creator, Redeemer and Lover of our souls has made an eternal covenant with us: "I will be Your God, you will be My people." That is how God puts it in all the covenants of grace. All that God is, God places at our disposal. And the blood of Jesus Christ forever seals that commitment, that covenant. So the Apostle Paul, in Romans again, can reason from the cross to hope for everyday living. He writes: "If God is for us, who is against us? He who did not spare His own Son, but delivered Him up for us all, how will He not also with Him freely give us all things?" (Romans 8:31–32). God has given us the best; can God not be trusted to provide us with the rest we need? That is the question I have to keep asking myself. If God has given me Jesus Christ, cannot God be trusted to give me all the rest of what I need? The Living God is Yahweh-*jireh*, Yahweh the Provider (Genesis 22:14).

The eighth commandment, therefore, calls us to once again bank our hope on Yahweh. The eighth commandment calls us back to the first commandment: "You shall have no other gods before me." The signs that we are banking our hope on Yahweh are (1) a freedom to protect our neighbor's property, a freedom to desire the best for our neighbor; and (2) a freedom to give to others.

Pastors are regularly under pressure, usually by the "stewardship" committee, to preach stewardship sermons—to at least once or twice a year preach on giving. A number of years ago I decided not to do so. Why? Because I am afraid to? Not at all! Then why not preach more often on giving? Because of the conviction that if I am not giving the resources entrusted to me it only reveals a deeper problem: I do not trust the God who loans me the resources. So instead of "hammering away" at giving, I "hammer away" on the goodness and faithfulness of God. For if I really do believe that the One who freely went to the cross for me can take care of me, then I will not be afraid to give myself away to Him and His purposes in the world. If we have been won by the love of God in Jesus Christ, we will want to give all we can to make sure other people get in on that love. Right? If we have tasted the sweetness of the Bread of Life, we will want to share it with others who hunger for something more.

Instead of the exhortation "give", Scripture exhorts us "once again to bank on the goodness and faithfulness of the God who comes to us in Jesus Christ". Hands reaching up and clinging to Him no longer cling to anything else!

When Sharon and I were married in 1971, we prayed a prayer that helps us in the journey of trust. We commend it to you. The prayer comes out of a right understanding of the intent of the eighth commandment. It is recorded in Proverbs 30:7–9:

> Two things I ask of You,
> Do not refuse me before I die:

Keep deception and lies far from me, and
Give me neither poverty nor riches.
Feed me with the food that is my portion,
Lest I be full and deny You and say 'Who is Yahweh?'
Or lest I be in want and steal,
And profane the name of my God.

EXODUS 20:16

"You shall not bear false witness."

THE TRUTH WILL SET YOU FREE

At the end of World War II, Elton Trueblood, a prolific Quaker philosopher/theologian, wrote a book on the Ten Commandments entitled, *Foundations for Reconstruction*. He was asking, after the defeat of the forces of oppression, how now does the world live together? Trueblood argued that in the Ten Commandments—in the Law given to Moses—the Eternal God has laid out a solid foundation for a free and just society. In the Commandments, the Manufacturer has laid out the foundations for a righteous life, a life rightly-related to God and rightly-related to one another.

"You shall not bear false witness."

Why does God put it in the negative? Why does he say, "You shall not bear false witness"? Why not put it positively, "You shall bear true witness on behalf of your neighbors"? Because as Martin Luther says in his *Larger Catechism*: "...it is a common evil plague that everyone prefers hearing evil to learning good from his neighbor." Need I illustrate? Luther continues: "...And although we ourselves are so bad that we cannot suffer that anyone should say anything bad about us, but everyone would much rather that all the world should speak of him in golden terms, yet we cannot bear that the best is spoken about others."

Luther is right, isn't he? So the Protector of our lives has to put it the way we have it in the Law: "You shall not bear false witness against your neighbor."

The Lawgiver experienced the disobedience of the ninth commandment first-hand when He became one of us. Jesus, *Y'shua*, Yahweh-to-the-Rescue, experienced people bearing false witness against Him throughout the whole of His earthly life. False things were said about the circumstances of His conception and birth. False things were said about His character. False rumors were spread about what He said in His sermons, and it all culminated in His trial where the court listened to no one but false witnesses.[1]

"You shall not bear false witness against your neighbor."

The question is, why is this included in the ten "Foundations for Reconstruction"? It is clearly an important issue. But is it really important enough to be included in "The Big Ten"? What is the big deal? Why include a commandment about verbal offense against others along with clearly essential matters like not taking another's life, or spouse, or property?

For two fundamental reasons. One, false witness—untruth— destroys the community. Two, false witness—untruth—goes against the character of God, and thus against the grain of our humanity as created in the image of God.

---

1 See Mark 14:55ff.

1. The ninth commandment has to be included in the good Law because false witness, untruth, is a hungry termite eating away at the fiber of relationships.

That was the great tragedy of the Watergate crisis of the early 1980's in the United States. The nation was never so close to collapse as it was during those dark days. Who were we to believe? Who was telling the truth? John Dean? The reporters working for the *Washington Post*? Senators Sam Erwin and Howard Baker? President Nixon? We who lived through that crisis felt profoundly insecure thinking our President was lying to us. I remember the relief nearly everyone felt when Gerald Ford became President. He may not have had all of the skill and experience we wanted in a President, but he did have integrity. We could trust him to say what he meant and mean what he said.

Charles M. Swezey, then Professor of Ethics at Union Theological Seminary in Virginia, argued that not bearing false witness is "a precondition for order in society.... Life is not possible without a minimal trust in the veracity of words.... The institutionalization of this practice is a social condition for the survival of society."[2] The promise to "tell the truth, the whole truth, and nothing but the truth" is absolutely critical for a just society. It is absolutely critical for any healthy, giving relationship.

The original setting in which Yahweh spoke the ninth commandment was the courtroom. Each of the Hebrew words in the commandment are technical legal terms—*ed sheqer. Ed* means "evidence," as in presenting evidence during a trial. *Sheqer* means "false, fraudulent, deceiving," in the sense of "groundless,

---

2 Charles M. Swezey, *Interpretation*, Vol. XXXIV. No.4 (October 1980) 407.

without basis in fact or reality."[3] In the ninth commandment, the Judge of all the earth, the Judge of every woman and man, is telling us that justice, and therefore authentic freedom, is subverted by false witnessing.

Because the Judge knows our hearts—that is, as Martin Luther said, that we naturally latch on to negative reports about others—Yahweh had Moses set up three safeguards for the judicial process; three safeguards to help people think twice about giving false witness in the courtroom:

(A) First, there was the stipulation that a person's testimony had to be confirmed by two or three other witnesses (Deuteronomy 19:15). God knows that we are more likely to tell the story straight in the presence of others who also know it. As we see in the four Gospels, Jesus affirms this stipulation. In Matthew 18:16, for instance, Jesus quotes Deuteronomy 19:15: "By the mouth of two or three witnesses every word may be confirmed." Jesus even submits His own testimony to this stipulation. In the fifth chapter of the Gospel according to John, Jesus summons four witnesses to substantiate His claim to have the authority to heal on the Sabbath (John 5:33–47).

But what about the possibility that the two or three other witnesses are lying?

(B) The second safeguard: if a witness is proved false (to have lied), the witness is to receive the punishment he or she wanted for the person he or she lied about (Deuteronomy 19:19). So if my false testimony sends you to jail, and if my lie is later discovered, I must go to jail and serve the time to which the judge has

---

3 Robert P. Mills, *And God Spoke All These Words: The Ten Commandments for the Third Millennium*, (PLC Pub, 2000).

sentenced you. Woe to me if I had lied at a trial of a person who received the death penalty!

(C) The third safeguard was even heavier. The witness became the executioner (Deuteronomy 17:7)! You can see the wisdom in this. For I would become a murderer if I lied. I live then with a doubly-burdened conscience: I lied, and I killed an innocent person. I wonder if our modern judicial systems would get to the real truth if we had safeguards like these?

Although the courtroom was the original setting for the ninth commandment, the rest of Scripture shows us that the intent of the commandment reaches beyond the legal realm, into every part of our lives. The fact is, we are "on trial" all the time and we put others "on trial" all the time. We are always being judged by others, and we are always judging others. The Czech scholar Jan Milic Lochman puts it this way: "Sometimes we ourselves are exposed to the accusation and condemnation of others; at other times, often without fully realizing it, we ourselves don the mantle of the prosecutor or even of the sentencing judge in the 'trial' of other people's lives."[4]

How often and quickly our behavior is wrongly interpreted by others, and how often and quickly we wrongly interpret the behavior of others. How often and quickly others think they understand our motives, but are wrong; and how often and quickly we think we understand others' motives, but are wrong. In the process our and others' reputations and dignity are damaged.

So in the rest of Scripture the Lawgiver extends the ninth

---

4 Jan Milic Lochman, *Signposts to Freedom: The Ten Commandments and Christian Ethics* (Minneapolis: Augsburg Publishing House, 1982), 139.

commandment beyond the literal courtroom into the "court-room" in which we live out all of our relationships. We, therefore, find tests like Leviticus 19:11: "You shall not lie to one another." And Leviticus 19:16: "You shall not go about as a slanderer. False witness not only subverts justice, but it strains relationships. Indeed, it can destroy persons: "With their mouths the godless destroy their neighbor" (Proverbs 11:9).

I remember as a child singing with my buddies, "Sticks and stones will break my bones, but names will never hurt me." Are you kidding? Names hurt us far deeper than sticks and stones: "Like a club and a sword and a sharp arrow is a man who bears false witness against his neighbor" (Proverbs 25:18).

Bearing false witness takes on all kinds of forms. Clearly it can involve outright lies. But it can also involve the "innocent" passing on a story about another person without first checking out the facts. I'm afraid that happens in churches all too frequently. I have done it. Assured that the facts shared with me were all of the facts, I then make a judgment too quickly and end up very ashamed. How many people have been hurt by false rumors? Or hurt by true rumors that ought not be passed on?

There are even more subtle ways to bear false witness. The classic is by inference, that is, by leaving a false impression.[5] You know what I mean: "Say Joe, notice how much better dressed old Pete is since he became City Treasurer?" Or, "Gee, Bob has spent a lot of time with Sally lately. She sure is beautiful." Such off-the-cuff comments spawn suspicion; they plant seeds of distrust. In the church we have a way of justifying such bearing

---

5 I forgot who helped me see this; I want him or her to be acknowledged for the insight.

false witness. We say, "I thought you ought to know so you can join me in praying for Bob and Sally."

Another way we break the ninth commandment is by exaggerating. We stretch the truth to make the facts look better. The other side of this is telling half-truths, "innocently" leaving out certain details.

No matter how we lie, and no matter what form the lie takes, it destroys relationships and it destroys community. Relationships are built on trust. And trust requires telling the truth.

The Living God takes all of this very seriously. You remember the story in the book of Acts about Ananias and Sapphira? Many of the Christians in Jerusalem had sold their property and had given the proceeds to the church. Ananias and Sapphira sold a piece of property, but kept back some of the money for themselves. Ananias brought a portion of the money and laid it at the Apostle's feet. Then Peter said to him: "Ananias, why has Satan filled your heart to lie to the Holy Spirit? You have not lied to men, but to God" (Acts 5:3). When Ananias heard these words he fell dead.

Now we need to be clear about what happened. There was nothing wrong with Ananias and Sapphira keeping some of the proceeds of their sale of land for themselves. That was their rightful choice. The evil that Peter confronted in them was not their desire to keep the money. The evil was their telling the apostles and the church that they were giving it all. The evil was their deceit. Since deceit always ruins the community. It had to be renounced. If Ananias would not be honest then he had to be removed.

You may be asking yourself now, "Is it ever right not to tell the truth?" "Is there ever a time when to lie is the lesser of two evils?" Consider these two responses.

First, the end seldom justifies the means. We need to be very careful about excusing disobedience by appealing to the end accomplished by our disobedience. More often than not disobedience only breeds more disobedience. Unrighteousness does not accomplish the righteousness of God. To lie is to move into very dangerous territory—into the devil's territory. Jesus calls the devil, "the father of lies" (John 8:44). To lie is to begin playing the devil's game and, as John Stott says, "We will never beat the devil at his own game."[6]

Second, there are times when telling the whole truth is not the most helpful thing to do. Someone asks you about their appearance, about their new hair style, for instance. "How do you like the way I am doing my hair?" You think it is awful. Do you say so? "It's terrible. It makes you look like...well...."[7] Or more seriously, your friend's husband has been abusing her and her children. They have run to your house for protection. The husband comes to your house in a rage asking if his wife is in your house. Do you say, "Yes"?

Here is where the Apostle Paul's summary of the Law comes into play. In Romans he says: "Owe nothing to anyone except to love one another; for they who love their neighbors have fulfilled the law" (Romans 13:8). The point of the ninth commandment is to seek my neighbor's well-being. Seeking his or her well-being may require my being judicious with the whole truth.

In the hairstyle case, to tell the person it is awful could be very hurtful. I do not need to lie and say, "Oh, it's nice." I can say, "It

---

6 John R. W. Stott, *God's New Society: The Message of Ephesians* (Downers Grove: Inter-Varsity Press, 1979), 277.
7 Lewis Smedes, *Mere Morality*.

sure does make you feel good about yourself. I like that!" or, "I see you are learning to express yourself in new ways. I like that!" Or I could be wise enough to recognize that the question, "Do you like my hair?" is really the question, "Do you notice me?" And I honor the ninth commandment by saying, "It is really good to see you feeling happy today."

In the case of the angry husband, to tell him everything I know could be very harmful for his family and for me. In that case, I need to set the safety of the family over the man's desire to know all of the facts. Rahab, the harlot, is blessed by Israel and by God for not telling everything to the King of Jericho when he came looking for Jewish spies (Joshua 2).

The Apostle John says in the prologue to his Gospel, "The Law was given through Moses; grace and truth were realized through Jesus Christ" (John 1:17). Grace and truth. For Jesus it is never just truth. It is always truth and grace, grace and truth. Truth without grace can become oppressive legalism. Grace without truth can become sentimental relativism. Like Jesus, we need to stand not with one foot in grace and one foot in truth, but with both feet in grace and both feet in truth.

Falsehood destroys relationships. That is why the ninth commandment is in the Big Ten. But the opposite is also true. Truth builds up relationships. Paul writes in Ephesians: "We are no longer to be children, tossed here and there by waves, and carried about by every wind of doctrine, by the trickery of humans, by craftiness in deceitful scheming; but speaking the truth in love, we are to grow up in all aspects into Him [Christ]..." (Ephesians 4:14–15). Truth spoken in love builds up. Truth spoken in love sets free. That is the first reason Yahweh commands, "You shall not bear false witness."

2. The second reason is more critical, more fundamental. It is the character of God.

Like the other commandments in the Law, the ninth emerges from who God is. Yahweh is the true God and the God of truth (Psalm 33:4–5; Deuteronomy 32:4). Yahweh does not lie. Indeed, Yahweh cannot lie (Titus 1:2; Numbers 23:19). To lie would go against God's very being. Thank God! So Jesus calls Himself, "the way, and the truth, and the life" (John 14:6). Jesus calls the Holy Spirit, "the Spirit of truth" (John 14:17).

The phrase "God is light" gets to the point best. Falsehood always seeks some measure of darkness. Falsehood always seeks, to some degree, to cover up or to hide. "God is light," says the Apostle John. God's very nature is light. "And in Him there is no darkness at all (1 John 1:5)." Darkness is the complete anti-God state of being; the lie is the anti-God state of mind. Jesus refers to Satan as "...a liar, and the father of lies" (John 8:44).

Because God is light, God hates lies. We read in Proverbs:

> There are six things which Yahweh hates,
> Yes, seven which are an abomination to Him:
> Haughty eyes, a lying tongue,
> And hands that shed innocent blood,
> A heart that devises wicked plans
> Feet that run rapidly to evil
> A false witness who utters lies,
> And one who spreads strife among brothers.
>
> Proverbs 6:16–19

We read in the book of Psalms:

They who practice deceit shall not dwell within my house;
They who speak falsehood shall not be established before
my eyes.

Psalm 101:7

It is not surprising then to find Jesus directing His fiercest words against the hypocrites.[8]

The psalmist expresses the intent of the ninth commandment when he prays, "Behold [O God] You desire truth in the innermost being" (Psalm 51:6). The Living God lives in and out of a truthful center. The Living God calls us to live in and out of a truthful center.

The practical question is, therefore, "How?" How can I live in and out of a truthful center? How do I live in integrity?

(1) By biting my tongue! Remember what our parents used to say? "If you have nothing good to say, don't say anything at all." Before speaking, bite my tongue for fifteen or twenty seconds in order to think about what I am wanting to say. Is this true? Is this a helpful truth? The tongue reveals what is going on in the heart. But the tongue can also control what is going on in the heart. As Richard Foster puts it: "The tongue is a thermometer; it tells us our spiritual temperature. It is also a thermostat; it controls our spiritual temperature."[9] The Psalmist prays: "Set a guard, O Yahweh, over my mouth; keep watch over the door of

---

8 See Matthew 23: 13,14,23,25,27,29.
9 Richard Foster, *Celebration of Discipline: The Path to Spiritual Growth* (San Francisco: Harper & Row, 1988), 89.

my lips" (Psalm 141:3).

(2) I can live in and out of a truthful center by plugging my ears. Given our propensity to listen to negative reports about others, we should follow what Martin Luther is purported to have advised—"turn our ears into 'graves.'" We simply refuse to listen to the rumors, the innuendos or the gossip.

(3) I can live in and out of a truthful center by putting myself in the other person's shoes. How would I feel if the thing I want to say about the other were said about me? How would I feel if half-truths, or inconclusive reports or surmises were spoken about me? What am I doing then, preparing to speak less than the truth?

(4) Having bit my lip, plugged my ears, put myself in the other's shoes, I can try to get in touch with why the truth is not good enough. Why is it that I feel I must stretch or twist the truth? Is it because I have been hurt and want to get even? Is it because I am angry? Often lying comes out of an inadequate view of self. I am insecure, so I exaggerate to prop up my ego. That may even involve lying about a coworker to pull her down so I look better. Or am I self-righteous, so I feel I have the right to judge and spread my "verdict" throughout the community? Or am I fearful? If the boss knew the truth—even absolute truth—she would fire me. So I changed the facts to save my job.

Of course you realize what else I am doing here, do you not? I am saying that God is not big enough to protect me if the truth were known. *I have to help God out by manipulating the facts.*

So, if the truth is not good enough for me, before opening my mouth I need to try to get in touch with why it isn't good enough; and then deal with myself at that more basic level.

(5) I live in and out of a truthful center by coming to the light. By coming into the presence of the Light of the World Himself, and letting Him expose me to myself. Let Yahweh reveal my real motives. It is safe to do, for He only reveals our sin in order to cleanse it, to melt it away.

Joy Davidman puts her finger on the real problem: "Greatest and first of a man's lies are usually those he tells about himself. Hitler could not have forced the 'big lie' technique down the throat of Germany if he had not begun by lying about the goodness and wisdom of Hitler."[10] Our delusions about ourselves melt away in the presence of Jesus Christ, which is why many people resist Jesus. They cannot handle the light exposing the darkness of the human heart. As John says: "Everyone who does evil hates the light, and does not come to the light, lest their deeds should be exposed" (John 3:20). Jesus is a threat to us when we cling to any lie. But if we want to live from a truthful center, Jesus is a Savior.

When I dare to let Him tell me about myself this is what He says: (A) "Your heart is more deceitful than all else" (Jeremiah 17:9; see also Genesis 6:5). And He is right. Jesus does not play games with us. He tells it like it is. What He tells us about ourselves melts any self-righteousness or judgmental spirit. (B) But then, before His diagnosis of my heart causes me to despair, He says, "I love you. I died to forgive you. I have come to change your heart." "Amazing grace, how sweet the sound." "The Gospel says you are more sinful and flawed than you ever dared believe, yet you are more accepted and loved than you ever dared hope

---

10 Davidman, op.cit., 112.

because Jesus lived and died in your place."[11] I no longer need to hide from myself or hide from others or hide from God. I no longer need to cover up or exaggerate. I need no longer to pull others down to make me look good, for I am loved. The same light that exposes my deceitful heart loves me, and understands me, and forgives me, and sets me free.

And then the truth is good enough: "...If we walk in the light as God is in the light, we have fellowship with one another and the blood of Jesus cleanses us from all sin" (1 John 1:7).

We live in and out of a truthful center by consciously living every moment in the Presence of Jesus, the faithful and true witness.[12] Who breathes His Spirit of Truth into our hearts. Who in turn bears His faithful and true witness to Jesus, and enables us to bear our faithful and true witness to Him also.

As a result, we will find ourselves living out the positive form of the ninth commandment as we have it in Ephesians 4:29:

> Let no unwholesome word proceed from your mouth, but only such a word as is good for building up...that it may give grace to those who hear.

---

11 Peter Scazzero, *The Emotionally Healthy Church: A Strategy for Discipleship that Actually Changes Lives* (Grand Rapids: Zondervan, 2003), 81.
12 Revelation 1:5; 3:14; 19:11

A SOUL RUNNING ON EMPTY

"You shall not covet your neighbor's house; you shall not covet your neighbor's wife or his male servant or his female servant or his ox or his donkey..." or her new spring wardrobe or his new Lexus sports utility vehicle or her new Gateway computer or their vacation to the Bahamas or her new position in the company or his reputation...*"or anything else that belongs to your neighbor."*

When we lived in Glendale, California [1993-2000], at 6:57 a.m. every weekday morning, I listened to Michael Josephson (of the Josephson Institute of Ethics) on KNX radio. One morning he told a story, apparently true, that takes us to the heart of the tenth commandment. Two men who were business partners went on a gold-mining expedition. They found two hundred gold nuggets. On their way back one of the men fell, and he was injured so badly that he died. Just before dying he said to his partner, "Give my wife whatever you want." Of the two hundred gold nuggets, "Give my wife whatever you want." After the funeral for the man, the partner gave the man's wife one gold nugget. She was outraged, and somewhat confused about her husband's love for her. Why was he not more direct saying something like, "Give my wife fifty percent of what we found"? Why this "Give her whatever you want"? But she trusted that her husband had known what he was doing; she had known him to be a wise man. The case ended up in court, and was to be tried by a very strict judge who had a reputation for going by the letter of the law. This suited the living partner just fine; he reasoned that the judge would take the words, "Give her whatever you want," literally. After hearing all of the factors involved, the judge ruled that the partner had to give the man's wife one hundred and ninety-nine gold nuggets. "Why?" was the protest; he told me, "Give my wife whatever you want!" To which the judge responded, "That is exactly what I have ruled. You want one hundred ninety-nine gold nuggets. I am giving her whatever you want."

Up to this last line of the Law we might be able to say to ourselves, "Well, I may not be living the Law perfectly, but I'm not doing that badly." The last line ends the illusion: "You shall not covet...anything...that belongs to your neighbor."

The Apostle Paul was undone by the tenth commandment. In chapter seven of his letter to the believers in Rome, he is wrestling with the Law. He argues that the Law is good—as good as the God who spoke it. Why then, as he seeks to seriously live the Law, does he find himself sinning all the more? Is the Law to blame? No! The culprit is sin. The problem is that sin sneaks up alongside the Law and uses the Law to make sin even worse. "What shall we say then? Is the Law sin? May it never be! On the contrary, I would not have come to know sin except through the Law; for I would not have known about coveting if the Law had not said, 'You shall not covet.' But sin, taking opportunity through the commandment, produced in me coveting of every kind..." Then Paul says, "I was once alive apart from the Law; but when the commandment came, sin became alive, and I died..." (Romans 7:7–9). The tenth commandment made Paul see just how bad sin is and awakened even more sin in him.

Apparently, Paul once thought that he was doing very well before the Law. He writes in the third chapter of his letter to the believers in Philippi: "If anyone else has a mind to put confidence in the flesh, I far more: circumcised the eighth day, of the nation of Israel, of the tribe of Benjamin, a Hebrew of Hebrews; as to the Law, a Pharisee; as to zeal, a persecutor of the church; as to the righteousness which is in the Law, found blameless" (Philippians 3:4–6).

Blameless? Until the tenth commandment finally broke through, and he was leveled before the Law. And became all the more covetous. And knew that he needed a Savior.

As Jesus was making His way to Jerusalem a man encountered Him who asked, "Good Teacher, what shall I do to inherit eternal life?" One of the most important questions we can ever ask: "Good Teacher, what shall I do to inherit eternal life?" And Jesus said to him, "'Why do you call Me good? No one is good except God alone. You know the commandments, "Do not murder, Do not commit adultery, Do not steal, Do not bear false witness, Do not defraud, honor your father and your mother."' And he [the man] said to him, 'Teacher, I have kept all these things from my youth up'" (Mark 10:17–20).

Now notice. When Jesus lists the commandments He stops short of the last; He does not list "Do not covet."[1] Why? Why list only commandments five through nine—commandments that

---

1 It was Ronald Wallace who helped me see this for the first time.

are measured primarily in external ways? Why not list the tenth, the commandment that goes to the heart, to the heart behind commandments five through nine? Because, as long as Jesus stops short of the tenth commandment, the man can think that he has "kept all these things from my youth up."

Mark continues saying, "And looking at him, Jesus felt a love for him, and said to him, 'One thing you lack: go and sell all you possess, and give to the poor, and you shall have treasure in heaven; and come, follow Me'" (Mark 10:21). And Mark tells us that the man's face fell, and he walked away grieved, "for he was one who owned much property" (Mark 10:22).

What is going on here? Jesus lists the commandments but stops short of the tenth. The man says that he has kept the commandments Jesus lists. Then Jesus calls him to give up all he owns. *Is that not Jesus' way of bringing the man to the tenth commandment?* Is that not Jesus' way of helping the man realize that, as a matter of fact, he cannot claim to have kept the other commandments?

He clearly has not kept the first commandment, "You shall have no other gods before Me." For Yahweh is now standing before him, in the person of Jesus, Yahweh-To-The-Rescue, calling him to follow. But he cannot do it. Eternal life is found in relationship with God in Jesus, in relationship with the Lawgiver. Eternal Life Himself is calling the man to follow. But the man cannot do what he needs to do in order to follow. His possessions had become his god, his ground for security, and the basis of his identity. He could not leave the god who had come between him and the Living God.

If Jesus told us, you or me, to sell all that we have and give to the poor and follow Him into insecurity, could we do it?

"All these commandments I have kept from my youth up." "Sell everything and come follow Me into the Kingdom of God." And he walked away grieving. For he realized that he had not kept all of the commandments. For he could not do the one thing; he could not trust Jesus enough to follow Jesus into the unknown.

When we break the tenth commandment, "You shall not covet," we have already broken the first, "You shall have no other gods before Me." Or, as I should say, we break the tenth commandment because we break the first. Or, again, if we break the first commandment, we will *always* and *automatically* break the tenth.

First commandment: "You shall have no other gods before Me." In the first commandment the Living God is telling us something about ourselves which we would have never discovered on our own: namely, that we were not only made *by* Yahweh, but that we were made *for* Yahweh; we were made *by* God *for* God; we were made *by* the Trinity *for* the Trinity. We were created in such a way that only Yahweh can satisfy the longings of our heart. When we break the first commandment, when we allow anyone or anything else to come between us and the Living God, our hearts begin to crave anything that promises to satisfy us.

Break the first commandment and we always and automatically break the tenth. We become souls running on empty, desiring anything and everything that can fill "the hole in the soul."

Is it any wonder that a post-Christian society like ours should increasingly become more and more materialistic, and more and more pleasure-oriented? Once we no longer find our satisfaction in God, we try to find it anywhere and everywhere else.

The title of an editorial in the *Los Angeles Times* said it so well:

"Life, Liberty and the Pursuit of Cheap Stuff."[2]

The fact is that when we break the first commandment, we not only always and automatically break the tenth, but we always and automatically also break the second through the ninth commandments. When the Living God is no longer the center of our lives we crave anything and everything to fill the void. We then break the second commandment, we begin to create God in our own image, we begin to create a God who fits into our understanding of reality. We then break the third commandment, we start to use God's name, the name Yahweh, in vain, using the name to try to get God to do our bidding. We then break the fourth commandment, we no longer stop the rat-race every seventh day, we no longer stop and seek the more of God which God only gives on the Sabbath. We then break the fifth commandment, we no longer honor our father and our mother, for to do so gets in the way of our quest for satisfaction. We then break the sixth commandment, maybe not by outright murdering someone, but we begin to harbor bitterness and anger which spill over in sarcasm and insult. We then break the seventh commandment, maybe not in literally committing adultery, in sleeping with someone to whom we are not married, but we begin to lust after another human being to fulfill our needs. We then break the eighth commandment, we begin to take what is not our own because we no longer trust God to provide for us. We then break the ninth commandment, we twist and manipulate the truth for our own advantage.

When we come, as we now have, to the end of the Law, we

2 Gary Hamel, "Life, Liberty and the Pursuit of Cheap Stuff." *Los Angeles Times*, 27 Mar. 2020.

are undone by the tenth commandment; and it makes us go back to the first and begin all over again.

Rene Girard, one of the most brilliant Christian thinkers of our time, suggests that commandments six through ten "prohibit the most serious acts of violence *in the order of their seriousness.*"[3] Coveting is the most serious form of violence? Girard goes on, "The verb 'covet' suggests that an uncommon desire is prohibited, a perverse desire reserved for hardened sinners. But the Hebrew term translated as 'covet' means just simply 'desire'. . .The desire prohibited by the tenth commandment must be the desire of all human beings – in other words, desire as such".[4] Desire as such is the most serious form of violence? Girard goes on, "If the Decalogue devotes its final commandment to prohibiting desire for whatever belongs to the neighbor, it is because it lucidly recognizes in that desire the key to the violence prohibited in the four commandments that precede it. If we ceased to desire the goods of our neighbor, we would never commit murder or adultery or theft or false witness. If we respected the tenth commandment, the four commandments that precede it would be superfluous".[5]

In his letter to the Colossians, Paul calls coveting idolatry: "Therefore consider the members of your earthly body as dead to immorality, impurity, passion, evil desire, and greed [or covetousness], which is idolatry" (Colossians 3:5).

Why? Why is coveting idolatry? Because, when we covet anything we do not have, our hearts are saying that God is not

---

3 Rene Girard, *I See Satan Falling Like Lightning* (Maryknoll, New York: Orbis Books, 2002), 7; emphasis mine.
4 Ibid, 7–8.
5 Ibid, 11–12.

good enough, we need more than what God in His goodness has given us. We need more than God.

Jeff Bjork, now retired Professor of Psychology at Fuller Theological Seminary, preached a sermon on the tenth commandment that he entitled, "The Heart of the Law." Jeff argues, rightly I think, that the Ten Commandments actually start and end on the same note. "Whereas the first commandment says, 'You will have no other gods before Me,' the tenth commandment hits the source of all such gods, and as such, it points out how we can avoid having any gods before our Lord." And what is that source? Ourselves. Myself. Yourself. When we no longer have the Living God as our God it does not mean we have no god. It means we make ourselves god. We make ourselves the god that is to be served. Everything is then seen from the perspective of how it is good for me. I am now the center of life. "Coveting occurs when we try to put ourselves in God's place at the center of our world." Which means, "Coveting is a sign against God, first and foremost." Coveting my neighbor's stuff is more of a sin against God than it is against my neighbor. For when I covet I have made myself the center of my world. All that matters is my need and its fulfillment.

There are two major Old Testament stories about the sin of coveting. One is about King Ahab, the other about King David. In 1 Kings 21, we read of Ahab's coveting the vineyard of Naboth. Ahab sends word to Naboth that he wants the vineyard. Naboth protests that it is his inheritance from his family. So Ahab, on advice from his wife Jezebel, devises a scheme by which Naboth is lied about and then murdered. In 2 Samuel 11, we read of David's coveting of the beautiful body of Bathsheba, Uriah's wife—David's neighbor's wife. David devises a plan to get her, which involves his lying to Uriah and then having him killed.

Both kings fall to their covetousness. Ahab, we expect to fall. He is evil to the core. David we do not expect to fall. He is, after all, "A man after God's own heart." But they both fall. Martin Luther thus argues, "This last commandment, then, is given not for rogues in the eyes of the world but precisely for the most pious who wish to be praised and to be called honest and upright people, since they have not offended against the former commandments."[6]

If we break the tenth commandment, it only means we have broken the first and will then break one or more of the other eight.

"You shall not covet...anything that belongs to your neighbor."

The tenth commandment was first spoken to people who were coming under the spell and pressure of Baal worship. Baal was the god of fertility, the god of pleasure, the god of wealth. "Baal was a covetous god."[7] Baal worship was fundamentally about coveting.

Are we not in the same place as those who first received the Law? Is Ronald Wallace too hard on us when he argues that our society "can only be kept going by the constant and fresh supply of a growing body of men and women who are geared into it by covetous desire and self-centered ambition"?[8] Is he too hard on us when he goes on to say, "To create demand for the products of this system we have to stimulate the desire to possess what it offers, and we do so by increasingly stimulating the appetite for possessions, and increasingly complicating the basic human

6 Quoted by Lochman, op. cit., 153.
7 Raymond Brown, *The Message of Deuteronomy: Not by Bread Alone* (Downers Grove, Illinois: Inter-Varsity Press, 1993), 91.
8 Wallace, op. cit., 178.

wants"?[9] A store advertises with the slogan, "For all the stuff you don't know you need."

Isn't the gambling craze driven by covetousness? Is not the out-of-control use of credit cards driven by covetousness? Credit cards "take the waiting out of wanting."[10] Have we not transformed what previous generations considered a vice into a virtue?

The Apostle James, two thousand years ago, explained the state of our society: "What is the source of quarrels and conflicts among you? Is not the source your pleasures that wage war on your members? You lust and do not have; so you commit murder. And you are envious and cannot obtain; so you fight and quarrel" (James 4:1–2). Singer/songwriter Rich Mullins hits the nail on the head:

> Everybody I know says they need just one thing.
> And what they really mean is that they need just one
>   thing more.[11]

The quest for more and more is the quest of souls running on empty—the quest of souls that have made themselves the center of their own universe and will never be satisfied.

The Catholic thinker Ronald Rolheiser makes a helpful observation:

> It is not an easy task to walk this earth and find peace. Inside of us, it would seem something is at odds with the very rhythm of

---

9 Ibid, 178.

10 Brown, op. cit., 91.

11 Rich Mullins, "My One Thing." *Rich Mullins.* Reunion Records, 1986.

things and we are forever restless, dissatisfied, frustrated, and aching. We are so overcharged with desire that it is hard to come to simple rest. Desire is always stronger than satisfaction.... We are driven persons, forever obsessed, congenitally diseased, living lives, as Thoreau once suggested, of quiet desperation, only occasionally experiencing peace. Desire is the straw that stirs the drink.... Spirituality is, ultimately, about what we do with that desire. What we do with our longings, both in terms of handling the pain and the hope they bring us, that is our spirituality.[12]

When we do not have the Living God as our god, when we no longer have Yahweh as the Infinite Center of our lives—as our all-consuming passion—two things happen. (1) First, we create a hole in the soul, a huge hole, a gaping hole, a God-sized hole. (2) And second, we become addicted to whatever it is we use to fill the hole.

In his extremely helpful book, *Addiction and Grace*, Psychiatrist Gerald May claims,

To be alive is to be addicted, and to be alive and addicted is to stand in need of grace.... After twenty years of listening to the yearnings of people's hearts, I am convinced that all human beings have an inborn desire for God. Whether we are consciously religious or not, this desire is our deepest longing and our most precious treasure. It gives us meaning. Some of us have repressed this desire, burying it beneath so many other interests that we are completely unaware of it. Or we may

---

12 Ronald Rolheiser, *The Holy Longing: The Search for a Christian Spirituality* (New York: Doubleday, 1999), 1.

experience it in different ways—as a longing for wholeness, completion, or fulfillment. Regardless of how we describe it, it is a longing for love. It is a hunger to love, to be loved, and to move closer to the Source of love. This yearning is the essence of the human spirit; it is the origin of our highest hopes and most noble dreams.[13]

Dr. May goes on to acknowledge that this desire is God given. And to acknowledge that something has gone wrong. "The longing at the center of our hearts repeatedly disappears from our awareness, and its energy is usurped by forces that are not at all loving. Our desires are captured, and we give ourselves over to things that, in our deepest honesty, we really do not want."

May then argues that the forces working against our deepest desires are repression and addiction. "We all suffer from both repression and addiction. Of the two, repression is by far the milder one." Repression we understand:

We frequently repress our desire for love because love makes us vulnerable to being hurt. The word *passion*, which is used to express strong loving desire, comes from the Latin root *passus*, which means "suffered." All of us know that, along with bringing joy, love can make us suffer. Often we repress our desire for love to minimize this suffering. This happens after someone spurns our love; we stifle our desire, and it may take us a long time before we are ready to love again. It is a normal

---

13 Gerald May, *Addiction and Grace* (San Francisco: Harper & Row, 1988), 1. This is the only book I am tempted to tape onto my Bible as "further revelation"—it captures the message of the Bible as no other book does for me!

human response; we repress our longings when they hurt us too much. Perhaps it is not surprising, then, that we do the same with our deepest longings for God. God does not always come to us in the pleasant ways we might expect, and so we repress our desire for God.[14]

But, argues May, repression is not as "vicious" as addiction. Here I am simply going to quote him at length; I do not want to lose the punch through my paraphrasing him.

The Paradoxes of Addiction

For generations, psychologists thought that virtually all self-defeating behavior was caused by repression. I have now come to believe that addiction is a separate and even more self-defeating force that abuses our freedom and makes us do things we really do not want to do. While repression stifles desire, addiction *attaches* desire, bonds and enslaves the energy of desire to certain specific behaviors, things, or people. These objects of attachment then become preoccupations and obsessions; they come to rule our lives.

I am not being flippant when I say that all of us suffer from addiction. Nor am I reducing the meaning of addiction. I mean in all truth that the psychological, neurological, and spiritual dynamics of full-fledged addiction are actively at work within every human being. The same processes that are responsible for addiction to alcohol and narcotics are also responsible for addiction to ideas, work, relationships, power, moods, fantasies, and an endless variety of other things. We are all addicts in every

---

14 Ibid, 2.

sense of the word. Moreover, our addictions are our own worst enemies. They enslave us with chains that are of our own making and yet that, paradoxically, are virtually beyond our control. Addiction also makes idolaters of us all, because it forces us to worship these objects of attachment, thereby preventing us from truly, freely loving God and one another. Addiction breeds willfulness within us, yet, again paradoxically, it erodes our free will and eats away at our dignity. Addiction, then, is at once an inherent part of our nature and an antagonist of our nature. It is the absolute enemy of human freedom, the antipathy of love. Yet, in still another paradox, our addictions can lead us to a deep appreciation of grace. They can bring us to our knees.[15]

Of course. And thanks be to God. For only God can finally free us from covetous hearts. That is, only God can recreate our hearts. And THAT is precisely what God promises to do!

"I will put my law within them, and in their heart I will write it."

Jeremiah 31:33

"I will give you a new heart and put a new spirit within you."

Ezekiel 36:26

And here is the wonder of grace. The Lawgiver does this by coming to dwell *in* our hearts! Can you imagine that? The one against whom we sin comes to take up residence *in* our sinful hearts! Yahweh-To-The-Rescue comes to live *in* our covetous hearts.

---

15 Ibid, 2, 5.

Thus the boldest prayer in the Bible: I ask the Father "to grant you, according to the riches of His glory, to be strengthened with power through His Spirit in the inner person; so that Christ may dwell in your hearts through faith." Glory! Christ, the Lawgiver dwelling in our hearts. The prayer continues, "And that you, being rooted and grounded in love, may be able to comprehend with all the saints what is the breadth and length and height and depth, and to know the love of Christ which surpasses knowledge, that you may be filled up to all the fullness of God" (Ephesians 3:16–19).

Glory, glory, glory!

The Lawgiver's response to our turning away from Him as the Infinite Center of Life is to come down from the mountain top and move into our hearts filling them with Himself! For unless He fills us, we will covet anything and everything that promises to fill the space meant only for the Triune God.

So where do we go from here? How do we obey the tenth commandment, and thus the first?

(1) First, we redirect the cravings. We reorient the longings. All of our cravings are symptoms of the deeper craving for God. All of our longings are symptoms of the deeper longing for God and His Kingdom.

> As the deer pants for the water brooks,
> So my soul pants for You, O God.
> My soul thirsts for God, for the living God.
>
> Psalm 42:1–2

Someday we are really going to get this. All of our pantings are symptoms of our panting for God. All of our hunger and thirst are symptoms of our hunger and thirst for God. "Seek first the kingdom of God and His righteousness," Jesus tells us (Matthew 6:33). He is calling us to redirect all of our anxiety about what we will eat, what we will drink, what we will wear, into "anxiety" to find God and the Kingdom.

"Seek first." The actual verb Jesus uses is elsewhere translated "persecute." It is a passionate verb. "Go hard after God," Jesus is saying. When everyone else is "going hard after" food and drink and clothing and status and security, you "go hard after" God and God's Kingdom. *That* is what we were made for. We will be satisfied with nothing less.

"I am the bread of life," claims Jesus. "I am that without which you cannot live. Eat all the other breads you can get your hands on. You will still be running on empty." "I am the bread of life; whoever comes to Me shall not hunger, and whoever believes in Me shall never thirst" (John 6:35). He is saying to us, "Redirect your cravings, reorient your longings. Your cravings are symptoms of your cravings for Me. Your longings are symptoms of your longings for Me. Seek Me and you will be too full to seek what a society running on empty seeks."

(2) Second, we obey by giving away as much as we can. By deciding that our society is buying a lie: the lie that we need all this stuff we have, and need all the stuff seductively advertised day and night. Fact of life: we do *not* need all this stuff. We need Christ. We need the things of the Kingdom. So, decide to give away as much as we can.

In his farewell address to the elders of the Church of Ephesus, Paul says, "I have coveted no one's silver or gold" (Acts 20:33). He then quotes Jesus saying, "It is more blessed to give than to receive" (20:35). Give. It is a powerful antidote to covetousness.

Yes, we give because others are in need. But *we give because we are in need.* We need to give so that our souls do not try to live the illusion that "all this stuff" heals the hole in the soul. Jesus asks us: "What does it profit you to gain the whole world, and forfeit your soul?" (Mark 8:36). I think it was the missionary Jim Elliot who said, "He is no fool who gives up what he cannot keep to gain what he cannot lose." Sacrificial generosity saves our souls.

Give away as much as we can. Need less in order to be more.

(3) Third, we obey by worshiping the Living God with all of our hearts, all of our mind, all of our soul, all of our strength. Someone has rightly said that to worship is to *feast on God.* To worship is to open our empty souls for God to fill them again with Himself. "What is the chief end of humanity?" asks the Westminster Catechism. The answer: "The chief end of human-ity is to glorify God and enjoy Him forever." I agree with those who argue that the Biblical answer is, "The chief end of humanity is to glorify God *by* enjoying God forever."

John Piper has demonstrated that we most honor God by enjoying God.[16] Not just giving God a salute—even a hearty salute. Not just giving God a tip—even a generous tip. We most honor God when we enjoy God and when God becomes the greatest joy of our lives. When we enjoy the joy God has in being Father, Son and Holy Spirit. When we enjoy the joy God has in being God to us. When we enjoy the joy God has in being our Savior. When we enjoy the joy God has in being the satisfaction of all of our cravings and longings. "In Your presence is full-ness..." "Fullness of joy; in Your right hand there are pleasures

---

16 John Piper, *The Pleasures of God* (Portland, Oregon: Multnomah Press, 1991), 1.

forever" (Psalm 16:11). "They drink their fill of the abundance of Your house; and You give them to drink of the river of Your delights" (Psalm 36:8).

The most powerful antidote to covetousness is to worship. Not just on Sundays, but every day. Stepping out of the center of the universe into the Infinite Center of Life who fills us again and again with His very life.

Many financial planners and weight-control coaches encourage us to *never* go to the market or to a restaurant without *first* drinking an eight-ounce glass of water; it helps us check our cravings. The Ten Commandments encourage us to *never* go into the day without *first* drinking our fill of the Living God; it keeps our cravings and longings in check and on track.

The tenth commandment brings us back to the first commandment. The tenth commandment calls us from the far country of emptiness to our home of fullness in the Trinity.

I can think of no more appropriate way to conclude this chapter and the whole book than with what John Piper wrote in the introduction to his book, *The Pleasures of God*. He dedicated the book to his four sons, and writes what I want to say to my children and to you.

> Finally, a word to my sons. The book is dedicated to you, Karsten and Benjamin and Abraham and Barnabas. If there is any legacy I want to leave you, it is not money or house or land; it is a vision of God—as great and glorious a God as one could ever see. But more than that, I want to leave the legacy of passion for this God. A passion far beyond what any human can produce. A passion for God flowing from the very heart of God. Never forget that God is most glorified in you when you are most satisfied in

him. But even more—and this is my prayer for you—in God's time, may your satisfaction in him be without measure, as it becomes the very pleasure of God in God.[17]

The Giver of the Ten Commandments says to you this day, "I am Yahweh your God, Who brought you out of the land of slavery. Go, live in the freedom for which I created you and am redeeming you."

---

17 Ibid, 11.

ACKNOWLEDGEMENTS

As you may have noticed, I have had many "teachers" as I have sought to understand and live the Ten Commandments. I have tried to carefully acknowledge the source of every idea and wording. Where I have not been successful I ask forgiveness.

Much of the material in this book was preached for the congregation of Glendale Presbyterian Church, January through April of 2000. I am very grateful to Judy Anderson, who served me as secretarial assistant at the time, for taking my handwritten notes (not easy to read!) and typing them into a form to which I have been able to easily add over the past years. Rev. John D'Elia graciously took the time to put together a bibliography to which I was also able to subsequently add. Any errors in either the chapters or the bibliography are, of course, mine.

I want to thank my colleagues at CCLN for their help in preparing this work for publication. Chris Price, for reading the text for theological accuracy and cultural connectivity. Josh Thompson for heading up the final editing process, alongside Jaden Neufeld. Daniel Roe for suggesting the title of the book;

so much better than what I proposed. And Arielle Ratzlaff on her beautiful design for the book. It is such a joy to work with committed, creative, and efficient disciples of Jesus.

The person who has helped me the most in the journey of understanding the Ten Commandments is Dr. Daniel P. Fuller, Professor Emeritus at Fuller Theological Seminary in Pasadena, California, U.S.A. It was he who first argued that we must not separate Law and Grace, for the giving of the Law is itself Grace, and it is Grace that, far from negating Law, enables the living of the Law. It was Dan Fuller who first taught us what should have been, and now is, obvious: the Giver of the Law is the Redeemer, the Redeemer is the Giver of the Law. It is, therefore, with profound gratitude that I dedicate this book to him.

BIBLIOGRAPHY

Bientenhard, Hans. "onoma". *Theological Dictionary of the New Testament, Vol. V*, ed. G. Kittel, trans. G. Bromiley. Grand Rapids: Eerdmans, 1967.

Bonhoeffer, Dietrich. *Life Together.* San Francisco: Harper & Row, 1954.

Bonhoeffer, Dietrich. *The Cost of Discipleship.* New York: Simon and Schuster, 1995.

Brown, Raymond. *The Message of Deuteronomy: Not by Bread Alone.* Downers Grove, Illinois: Inter-Varsity Press, 1993.

Bruner, Frederick Dale. *The Christbook: A Historical/ Theological Commentary: Matthew 1–12.* Waco: Word Books, 1987.

Buechner, Frederick. *Wishful thinking: A Theological ABC.* New York: Harper & Row, 1st Edition, 1973.

Chesterton, G. K. *The Everlasting Man.* San Francisco: Ignatius

Press, 1993.

Childs, Brevard S. *The Book of Exodus: A Critical, Theological Commentary.* Philadelphia: Westminster Press, 1974.

Cole, Alan. *Exodus: An Introduction and Commentary.* Downers Grove, Illinois: Inter-Varsity Press, 1973. (Tyndale Old Testament Commentaries Series).

Dawn, Marva. *Unfettered Hope: A Call to Faithful Living in an Affluent Society.* Louisville: Westminster John Knox, 2003.

Davidman, Joy. *Smoke on the Mountain: An Interpretation of the Ten Commandments.* Philadelphia: Westminster Press, 1954.

Foster, Richard J. *Celebration of Discipline: The Path to Spiritual Growth.* San Francisco: Harper & Row, 1988.

Foulkes, Francis. *The Letter of Paul to the Ephesians: An Introduction and Commentary,* 2nd edition, Grand Rapids, Michigan: Eerdmans, 1989.

Fretheim, Terence E. *Exodus.* (Interpretation Series, A Bible Commentary for Teaching and Preaching). Louisville: John Knox Press, 1991.

Girard, Rene. *I See Satan Falling Like Lightning.* Maryknoll, New York: Orbis Books, 2002.

Hauck, Friedrich. "pornea". *Theological Dictionary of the New Testament.* Vol. VI, ed.G.Kittel, trans. G. Bromiley. Grand Rapids: Eerdmans, 1968.

Hybels, Bill. *Honest to God?: Becoming an Authentic Christian.*

Grand Rapids: Zondervan, 1992.

Jewett, Paul King. *The Lord's Day: A Theological Guide to the Christian Day of Worship*. Grand Rapids: Eerdmans, 1971

Jones, E. Stanley. *Christ of the Mount: A Working Philosophy of Life*. New York, Cincinnati [etc.]: The Abingdon Press, 1931.

Kittel, Gerhard. "doxa". *Theological Dictionary of the New Testament*, Vol. II, ed. G. Kittel. Grand Rapids: Eerdmans, 1964.

Lapide, Pinchas. *The Sermon on the Mount, Utopia or Program for Action?* Maryknoll, NY: Orbis Books, 1986.

Lochman, Jan Milic. *Signposts to Freedom: The Ten Commandments and Christian Ethics*. Minneapolis: Augsburg Publishing House, 1982.

Lohse, Eduard. "sabbaton". *Theological Dictionary of the New Testament*. Vol. VII. Ed. G. Kittel, trans. G. Bromiley. Grand Rapids: Eerdmans, 1971.

Malina, Bruce J and Richard L. Rohrbaugh. *Social Science Commentary on the Synoptic Gospels*. Minneapolis: Fortress Press, 1992.

May, Gerald G. *Addiction and Grace*. San Francisco: Harper & Row, 1988.

Mickey, Paul A. *Tough Marriage*. Grand Rapids: Pyrenees Books, 1990.

Morris, Leon. *The First Epistle of Paul to the Corinthians; An Introduction and Commentary*. (The Tyndale New

Testament Commentaries Series) Grand Rapids, Eerdmans, 1958.

New Bible Commentary: 21st Century Edition. Consulting editors, D. A. Carson et al. Downers Grove, Ill: Inter-Varsity Press, 1994.

The New International Dictionary of New Testament Theology (TDNT). Colin Brown, general editor. Grand Rapids, Mich.: Regency Reference Library, 1986.

Packer, J. I. *A Quest for Godliness: The Puritan Vision of the Christian Life.* Wheaton, Ill: Crossway Books, 1st edition, 1990, paperback 1994.

Packer, J. I. *I Want to Be a Christian.* Wheaton, Illinois: Crossway Books, 1994.

Packer, J. I. *Knowing God.* Downers Grove: Inter-Varsity Press, 1973.

Percy, Bernard, editor. *How to Grow a Child: A Child's Advice to Parents.* Los Angeles: Price/Stern/Sloan, 1978.

Piper, John. *The Pleasures of God.* Portland, Oregon: Multnomah Press, 1991.

Plantinga, Cornelius, Jr. *Not The Way It Is Supposed To Be: A Breviary of Sin.* Grand Rapids: Eerdmans, 1995.

Rolheiser, Ronald. *The Holy Longing: The Search for a Christian Spirituality.* New York: Doubleday, 1999.

Schimmel, Solomon. *The Seven Deadly Sins: Jewish, Christian, and Classical Reflections on Human Nature.* New York: The

Free Press (A Division of Macmillan, Inc.), 1992.

Schlessinger, Laura. *The Ten Commandments: The Significance of God's Laws in Everyday Life.* Thorndike, Maine: Thorndike Press, 1999.

Sider, Ronald J. *Rich Christians in an Age of Hunger: A Biblical Study.* Downers Grove, Illinois: Inter-Varsity Press, 1984.

Smedes, Lewis B. *Sex for Christians: The Limits and Liberties of Sexual Living.* Grand Rapids: Eerdmans, First edition, 1976.

Smedes, Lewis B. *Mere Morality.*

Stott, John R. W. *Christian Counter-Culture: The Message of the Sermon on the Mount.* Downers Grove: Inter-Varsity Press, 1978.

Tasker, R. V. G. *The General Epistle of James, An Introduction and Commentary.* Grand Rapids: Eerdmans, 1957.

Trueblood, Elton. *Foundations for Reconstruction.* New York, London: Harper & Brothers, 1946.

Vanauken, Sheldon. *A Severe Mercy.* San Francisco: Harper & Row, 1977.

Von Rad, Gerhard. *Old Testament Theology, Vol. 1.* Translated by D. M. G. Stalker. Edinburgh: Oliver and Boyd, 1962.

Von Rad, Gerhard. "doxa". *Theological Dictionary of the New Testament,* Vol.I. ed.G. Kittel. Grand Rapids: Eerdmans, 1964.

Wallace, Ronald S. *The Ten Commandments: A Study of Ethical*

Freedom. Grand Rapids, Mich.: Eerdmans, 1965.

Willard, Dallas. *The Divine Conspiracy: Rediscovering Our Hidden Life in God*. HarperSanFrancisco, 1998.

Zimmerli, Walther. *Old Testament Theology in Outline*. Atlanta: John Knox Press, 1978.